THE MIRROR EFFECT

MORE THAN SOUL MATES

THE MIRROR EFFECT

6 Steps to Finding Your Magical Match Using Online Dating

Troy Pummill & Judy Day

with an Afterword by
Stefanie Elkin, MA, LMFT

Confluence Books
Ashland, Oregon

Confluence Books titles may be purchased for educational, business, or sales promotional use. For information, please write:
Special Market Department
Confluence Books
PO Box 3400
Ashland, OR 97520
Website: www.whitecloudpress.com

Cover design by Hot Stone Communications
Middle photo: "Hold Infinity In the Palm of Your Hands,"
  Reza Ali (www.rezaali.net)

Interior design by Confluence Book Services

Printed in the United States of America

Library of Congress Cataloging-in-Publication Data
Pummill, Troy.
The mirror effect : more than soul mates : 6 steps to finding your magical match using online dating / Troy Pummill & Judy Day.
  p. cm.
 ISBN 978-1-935952-69-5 (pbk.)
 1. Online dating. 2. Mate selection. 3. Interpersonal relations. I. Day, Judy. II. Title.
 HQ801.82.P86 2012
 306.730285--dc23
                  2012019058

CONTENTS

THE DREAM

Do you dare to dream of love?

When you think of finding your ideal love, do you even know what to dream? Although it isn't hard to imagine being incredibly happy or wealthy, who among us can claim to know the elements that describe the superlative relationship? Is it profound love? Amazing intimacy? Deep caring? A beautiful companion? A lifelong best friend? Is it being with someone who completely understands and accepts us for who we are? Or is it something much, much more? Our vision of perfect love is nothing more than a silhouette shrouded in haze, an outline vague and mysterious, unreal and unobtainable. But it doesn't have to be that way...

July 5, 2011

A year ago, I went to Paris to begin writing this book—a simple yet life-changing little book on finding love. iPad in hand, I happened upon a shady sidewalk table at Le Bourbon, a café across from the Assemblée Nationale. It was a Saturday, the business of government was closed, and my quiet, corner table was the perfect place to spin my tale—how a first date on a cold January night in 2008 profoundly changed my life. How it exploded everything I knew about relationships...and taught me what to dream.

I can still remember that January night. As I sat across from my date, it became clear that she was very much like me. We thought alike, felt the same way about things, and shared a similar past. In mere minutes we began to feel like we had known each other forever. The gravity of our connection was palpable and deep.

As the evening progressed, I began to recognize a *pattern*—one impossible to miss after a 25-year career analyzing the patterns in computer communications. Our incredible connection arose because she was a *reflection of me*—a mirror. The effect was absolutely astonishing, as was the simplicity of the pattern.

I had stumbled upon the holy grail—a pattern for *human* connections. Reflection…then connection…and gravity…then bond.

Could it be? If you took two other people, who also mirrored each other, and put them together, would that same connection happen again? Was there a principle behind this pattern? Could I develop a process to harness it? *Dare I even try?*

Could it be possible to engineer… *love*?

Yes, indeed, it was possible; I had just discovered *The Mirror Effect*.

Built on the premise that couples who are highly alike enjoy a rare, extraordinary relationship, The Mirror Effect is the principle behind a 6-step process that leads to compelling dates, deep love, and, ultimately, a relationship beyond your wildest imagination—your Magical Match.

We aren't waving wands here; we're *engineering matches*. Mirror relationships are easy and harmonious; they exist without the friction, work, and compromise we've been taught must accompany every relationship. No more. You and your Magical Match will share amazing love and deep harmony—and together, learn to dream.

As for me, walking around Paris that warm July day, I thought about my exploration of the Mirror Effect and about the love I had found and lost. I pondered how the journey had actually strengthened my determination and belief. I *knew* my Magical Match would be coming soon.

Seven days later, I met Judy.

Today, I find myself back at Le Bourbon, that same shady sidewalk café, once again seeking shelter from the Paris heat. But this time, Judy is here with me.

It's hard to imagine how my journey through July, Paris, Peter Frampton, two first dates, and the Mirror Effect would all lead to this amazing love. But now it is clear. Judy is my dream—my Magical Match.

And so, together, we dedicate this book to those who dare to dream. We dedicate it to love… and to those who search for it.

So let's begin. It is your turn to take the first steps towards fulfilling your deepest dreams. It's time for you to find your Magical Match!

With Love,
Troy and Judy

PART 1

UNDERSTANDING
THE MIRROR EFFECT

THE MIRROR EFFECT LAWS

A Manifesto for the Heart

1. **If it's work, it's wrong.** Let go of relationships that have friction or require compromise.

2. **A Mirror relationship is the most advanced relationship you can experience.** It's the Everest of Relationships—the ultimate in both risk and reward.

3. **The Mirror connection is an undeniable, incredible force.** The gravity of the connection is obvious and compelling. Lives are irrevocably, profoundly changed.

4. **Everything is opposite.** Compared to traditional relationships, everything in the Mirror relationship is opposite.

5. **You don't choose the relationship; the relationship chooses you.** You enter the restaurant strangers, and leave as a couple.

6. **People will believe that you've gone mad.** It will take time for people to understand (but eventually they will).

7. **The Law of Averages does not apply to the Mirror Effect.** Playing the numbers game is not part of the Mirroring Process. Mirroring is not about casting a wide net.

8. **Know yourself.** The search for a Mirror begins inside of you, not outside.

9. **Effort is required to find your Magical Match.** You must take action: emailing, phone conversations, IM, dating.

10. **Filtering is essential to harness the power of the Mirror Effect.** Actively exploring *within a pool of Mirrors* is the only path to finding your Magical Match.

11. **Every Mirror is the same, but also different.** Each Mirror you meet will be the same, yet unique. It's a Mirror Effect paradox.

12. **There are no Magical Matches in the "Dead Zone".** There are only near misses.

13. **You only get to discover if your partner is ready to be your Magical Match after you're already deeply involved.** The connection happens *very* quickly, much faster than you can recognize potential flaws.

14. **Sometimes love is not enough.** No matter how strong the bond, there are obstacles not even love can overcome.

15. **It's devastating to lose a Mirror relationship.** There is no way around it.

16. **You have many Mirrors.** You can have the relationship you want.

17. **Once you've experienced a Mirror relationship, nothing else will ever do.**

THE 6 STEPS TO FINDING YOUR MAGICAL MATCH

Like countless other frustrated daters, you've probably arrived at this book having tried everything and yet The One remains a figment of your imagination. Date after date, relationship after relationship, year after year, true love remains elusive. "Soul mate" has become a concept distant and vague, reserved only for the lines in a script or the rhythmic stanzas of a timeless love sonnet. It's the long-lingering whisper in your head, the thought as you drive in traffic, the wish that someone was there to curl up with at night. Even with expectation long passed, somewhere deep inside remains the will to keep going—a flicker of hope that it can *still* happen for you.

How exactly is an intelligent, experienced person supposed to go about finding love in today's world? We're led to believe that love is just supposed to happen, right? So we blindly move through dating and mating, believing that love will miraculously germinate, cultivate, magnetize, spiritualize, or materialize. *How crazy is that?* We're expected to pick a life partner based on *serendipity*? Is there *anything* else in life that functions similarly? Education? Career? Selecting a car? *Grocery shopping?!* Do we just wander down the grocery store aisles aimlessly picking up items in hopes they'll happen to make a great dinner? Or perhaps if we just write the perfect grocery list and meditate on it hard enough, the perfect meal will magically appear in our oven? Or on our doorstep?

Not a chance…

We *go* to the grocery store to select the items we want. And when we're serious about producing the best meal, we use a *recipe*—a formula for making the perfect dinner.

Why is food by the numbers, but love left to the stars? Is it logical to select food so carefully, yet leave something as monumentally important as picking a life partner to chance? *What if romance could be like groceries?* Imagine that! If online dating is just a different type of grocery store, why can't we simply shop for that quixotic love of a lifetime?

The hindrance is the lack of a *dating recipe*.

There are certainly *countless* books on finding love. Romantic stories like Elizabeth Gilbert's *Eat, Pray, Love* touch and inspire readers, but the portrayed path to finding love is never a reproducible formula—even if you are willing to travel through three continents, eat lots of pasta, learn to meditate, and visit a medicine man.

Much closer and cheaper than Bali is Amazon.com with its forest of how-to books on dating. If you read them closely, you'll see that these books aren't very formulaic either. Most of these traditional guides merely teach how to *attract* or *react*. What they don't give you is a step-by-step, here's-how-you-do-it. Instead, they instruct you how to be on your best behavior or compliment your date's clothes, in hopes of…what? *A second date?* That's weak! When absurd dating advice like, "Opposites attract" and "Better breath for better dates" leaves you still combing the aisle for the right book rather than walking the aisle to the altar, it is time for a mindset change!

What you need is a formula to precisely extract The One from the dating pool. That's right, a *formula*! It's about the *right* mindset and the *right* target. When we can precisely identify strong, potential matches, the need to attract and react is eliminated. In the face of a tangible process, traditional guides become superfluous.

Enter the Mirror Effect. Mirror Effect relationships consist of two people who mirror each another in every aspect of life, starting on the innermost levels and radiating outward. Mirror relationships are filled with happiness, amazing chemistry, and a connection deeper than either partner has ever known. Imagine how wondrous a relationship could be with someone who innately understands you, with whom you can be yourself—completely—and feel inspired to be even more. Ponder a relationship that is effortless, peaceful, and harmonious—a love bond that transcends words. And that's just the tip of the Mirror relationship mountain.

My discovery of the Mirror Effect started with a single profound, real-life experience. When I explored further, I discovered a predictable, repeatable pattern based upon pure mirrored reflections—reflections that produce relationships of *astonishing* peace and joy.

The 6 steps outlined in this book provide a clear formula for identifying your strongest Mirrors from the vast pool of online daters. The Mirroring Process creates a self-correcting progression that starts by transforming your dates into fulfilling, enriching, and exciting experiences and continues down a path towards selecting a life partner. No more wild goose chases or wasted evenings without connection, just a steady, logical approach to finding your Magical Match.

The rest of this book will give you detailed guidance through the 6 steps of the Mirroring Process, but for now, I want to give you a sense of the terrain:

Step 1. Mirror Profile: *It's not that the online dating tool is bad, we just don't know how to use it.* Online dating is probably the single greatest leap forward in finding love—ever. The reason we fail is that we have no idea how to use the online dating tool properly. Rather than an irrelevant list of the superficial, a profile should be a mirror reflection of your *core* elements; the elements that produce lasting, meaningful relationships. Only quality matches will recognize themselves in the mirror created by your profile's words; the rest will simply move on because your profile didn't strike a deep chord within them. This is a *good* thing and is one of the self-correcting elements of the Mirroring Process. (Don't worry if you don't know what to write, "Step 1: The Mirror Profile" on page 67 will guide you through the process of writing your Mirror Profile.)

Step 2. Filter: *The fewer, the better.* Unlike traditional dating, Mirroring is *not* a frantic race to play the odds. Magical Matchers date exclusively only those filtered through their Mirror Profile. The 6-Step Mirroring Process is about depth and quality, not quantity. There is no point in having countless bad dates to only find one or two *maybes*. With time and resources being so valuable, you cannot afford to date randomly or blindly. Your dating experiences will dramatically improve as you begin to date only those who are filtered through your Mirror Profile.

Step 3. Connection: *Connect at the soul from the very first date.* Mirroring and Filtering produce a pool of candidates with whom you will share a substantial connection. Connection is an incredibly powerful element. It brings two strangers together and allows them to identify, explore, and interact in remarkable ways. With Mirror connections, time is accelerated and barriers are broken down. Because of this, you'll have an opportunity to connect at the deepest levels from the first date.

Step 4. Selection: *A good match is more than good love; a great match is more than great love.* Selection is about more than whether you can fall in love, or how much you love. There are plenty of divorced couples who still love each other. Selection is about matching and knowing what to match. In a Mirror relationship, pheromones and falling in love are no longer the criterion by which we choose a partner.

Step 5. Letting Go: *If it's work, it's wrong*—the #1 rule in Mirror relationships. Traditionally, we're taught that an effortless relationship is a fallacy; we must *work* at our relationships in order to mold them into the relationship we really desire. So, rather than search for a better match, we cling to a mediocre relationship and then strive to improve it. But what if everything we've been taught is wrong? What if you could have a relationship that has no friction, compromise or work—a *magical* relationship?

Within a pool of *highly matched* Mirrors an elevated level of selectivity emerges. In order to narrow down to your Magical Match, you must learn to let go of the Mirrors who are near misses—the relationships that are *nearly* effortless.

Step 6. Commitment: *Make it a Mission*. As with any program, to fully benefit, you must wholeheartedly commit to the process—employ a Mirror Profile, date only those who pass through the filter, determine if there's a connection, select your best matches, and swiftly let go of *nearly* perfect relationships. By committing to the process, you *increase* your confidence and amplify the ability to meet and select your Magical Match.

That's all there is to it. No rituals, no prayers, no fantasies, no magic wands, tarot cards or star charts. Not even a lucky rabbit's foot. Just 6 steps to finding your Magical Match; a tangible, logical, simple, reproducible, effective process to help you find the love of a lifetime.

> *"We're wired so alike it creates the most beautiful harmony. Sometimes I feel like I'm the violin and he's the bow, and together…well, you know you can't have the music of the violin without the bow and the bow can't make music without the violin. It's like that—they only make the most beautiful sound when they're played together. And it's the same thing being with your Magical Match—it's the most delicious, satisfying experience I've ever had."—Renee*

If you are seeking a path to finding a relationship beyond your wildest dreams, the roadmap is in your hands.

3

TRADITIONAL RELATIONSHIPS

"This is what a relationship is. We average our misery."
–Dr. Lisa Cuddy (of the hospital drama "House M.D.")

And in those words is the definition of the quintessential traditional relationship. In place of the beautifully matched storybook romance stands a relationship propped up by self-help books, workshops, therapists, and counselors. We've learned to settle. In a bittersweet mix of love, caring, commitment, strife, confusion, anger, and pain, we clutch to seemingly loving relationships that simultaneously drive us to agony and despair. It is an exercise in duality, a two-sided relationship coin. Joy or tears, happiness or difficulty, for better or for worse—we are told we must settle and accept both sides of the coin. "Even with a little suffering, it's more good than bad," they say. "A long, fruitful relationship is the dividend of effort and patience. In the end, it's all worth it."

But is this sage advice? How did this come to be the accepted norm? By what laws of either nature or nurture is it decided we must *suffer* and *compromise* in our relationships?

WHERE DOES OUR INNATE UNDERSTANDING OF TRADITIONAL RELATIONSHIPS BEGIN?

One obvious answer is from our parents. Children start with a unique perspective into just one romantic relationship—their parents'. Most of our foundational understanding of relationships is cemented in what we experience vicariously through our parents, molded in an environment that is often very far from the perfectly matched coupling. Present and impressionable, we watch our parents as they love, compromise, adjust, quarrel, struggle, and make up—or divorce. In living with and observing this dance, the patterns become imprints in our minds as we head into our own relationships. We subconsciously accept their relationship paradigms, whatever they were, as the norm. When our relationships face difficulties, our ingrained childhood reactions prevail. We never even really question whether there is a different way of being, a way that's better.

The media is another pervasive influence in our developmental understanding of relationships. Television no longer portrays highly matched couples. The Brady's had a great marriage (other than never having sex). Mike and Carol's relationship was loving, harmonious—and incredibly dull. In the fast-paced world of five-second sound bites, viewers prefer the sizzle of ridiculous mismatches: Roseanne and Dan Conner, Al and Peggy Bundy, Sandra Bullock and Jesse James? Even when Hollywood produces a deep love screenplay, the story is so unreal that we perceive it as fantasy rather than *any* form of reality.

Finally, those who have reached the summit of enduring relationships often proclaim that we must accept love in whatever form it comes. We hear that deep love is a fairy tale that belies the true struggle-equals-success nature of *real* relationships. As these elder veterans are the only successful role models we have, we're obliged to believe the messenger. Their bottom-line eerily echoes the experts advice:

- You're not going to get everything you want, so settle for the important things.
- Relationships require work.
- Couples must learn the art of compromise.
- Arguments are part of a relationship. You must learn to argue fairly.
- You can't expect your marriage to be good all of the time.

- Relationships go through phases.
- It's unrealistic to feel "in love" all of the time.
- Love is a choice.

THE PATH TO THE ORANGES

After absorbing all of these contemporary influences comes the coup de grâce: no one trains us how to *pick* partners. The first 20 years of our lives are spent in tutelage on most every possible life subject—except educating our Pickers. Our mentors struggle to tenaciously warn of drugs, fast cars, loud music, bad influences, unplanned pregnancy, and a bevy of communicable diseases, yet not a single word on how to select a compatible mate.

And so our callow picker head-dives into the dating pool without a model for finding a highly compatible relationship. We're defeated before we even start. On the grand adventure, we date, we kiss, and we eventually marry based upon our childhood conditioning. In our heads we whisper that any relationship worth having requires a lifetime's struggle towards the sweet rewards that we imagine 50 years of marriage will bring.

But our romantic dream of Camelot is undone by our preconceptions. The common relationship wisdom has created an environment wherein mismatches are *normal*. The familiar idioms become our mantras. We *expect* friction. We *assume* fights are healthy. We *exercise* compromise. And, inexorably, *we accept that our mate will be, in at least some ways, mismatched*. It's a self-fulfilling prophecy. The moment we believe the mantra chant, our notions become reality. Without a successful model, we unwittingly marry Attila the Honey, and take the first steps down the road towards the Oranges.

Yes, *the Oranges*. We've all witnessed the Oranges at work. When a pothole becomes too large to ignore, two guys, dressed in the most hideous orange color man can invent, jump out and shovel some asphalt into the gaping street hole. With a couple taps of the shovel, they declare the job finished, admonishing that as thousands of cars roll over the patchwork, healing will come as the new pavement is forcefully packed into place. The problem is that the first hard rain inevitably loosens the asphalt, which is subsequently ejected, and the hole once again reappears.

Let's face it. We fall in love ignoring the signs that suggest unrest, marry despite blinding evidence to the contrary, and then end up needing self-help books, magazine articles, Dr. Phil, workshops, Marriage Encounter, therapists, counselors, church—an entire Orange infrastructure—to advise us on how to fill our self-created potholes and keep our broken, mismatched relationships alive.

WHAT'S BEHIND THE TRADITIONAL RELATIONSHIP PARADIGM?

Did you know that there are more single people today than there have ever been? Or that a recent study shows that 30% of divorced women who get married admit they *knew* that they were marrying the wrong man? Today the average marrying age is *30* and the divorce rate has reached over 50%—both statistics are at their highest levels in history. These statistics are interrelated; they are all an artifact of the traditional relationship and its deleterious construction.

Traditional relationships are outside→in in nature. Read almost any online dating profile and you'll see what's abundantly clear. Traditional profiles tend to be superficial—they focus on activities, likes or dislikes, life's simple pleasures or displeasures. Even the most inane items become matching criteria, like a shared interest in the mating frequency of the Scaly-breasted Wren Babbler (sadly, it's more often than many couples). That's the level at which traditional relationships form. Based upon little more than superficial commonality, we date and take the first steps towards the relationship.

Over time, the couple's superficial discovery extends inward, down towards the heart and soul. They may find one or two deeper compatibility elements—shared spirituality, mentality, or emotion-ality—but in the larger picture, the remaining mismatched elements are ignored as the relationship moves forward. The experts say that a prototypical traditional relationship is a two-year path of discov-ery—that's over a *million* minutes. And in each of those minutes resides not only the time to test compatibility, but also to absorb, rationalize, discount, and accept the mismatches in a relationship.

Let's take look at a typical American couple. Sarah is an interior designer in her 30s—bright, accomplished, respected in both art and business worlds. Tom is a firefighter. Tall, rough, and rugged. A thrill-seeker, Tom is always exciting to be around.

Sarah and Tom's relationship started five years ago with a bang—the kind that comes with bent fenders and an exchange of insur-ance information—and so began a relationship filled with beautiful love and so much potential. But now the luster has faded; Sarah and Tom argue more than love. Their mismatch does not surren-der to compromise—nor does it work. Sarah feels misunderstood, pressured, irritable, and angry. Tom feels exasperated, nagged, and physically unsatisfied.

Yet another trip to their therapist finds Sarah and Tom striving to identify the broken pieces of their pasts that they believe affect their ability to make their relationship work. But no matter how deeply they dig into their individual psyches, truly transforma-tive insights seem elusive. Any improvements in their relation-ship quickly evaporate, invariably returning to their intractable, argumentative state.

The sad thing about Tom and Sarah is that their circumstances—or ones like them—exist for millions of unhappy couples. Their is-sues are endemic to the progression traditional relationships take as they move from meeting through courtship to commitment:

- Due to the slow outside—in discovery, the deeper mis-matches go undiscovered until the relationship is well underway.

- The honeymoon phase covers up the friction while the mismatches become baked into the relational foundation.
- When the mismatches finally come to light, the nature of our understanding entices us to accept them as normal and to carry on, either choosing to work with the mismatches or to accept them as a point of contention.
- The setting of the honeymoon phase gives rise to the cool night. Without the warmth of fiery new love to smooth the underlying problems, all that remains is a mix of love's embers and friction.
- Finally, the traditional advice implores us to keep trying.

The warm, sunny days of infatuation and courtship shorten in an inevitable downward spiral from happiness to ambivalence to despair. And as you cry out that the relationship is suffocating your soul, the Oranges preach, "Love is a choice." True enough; however, what they are actually promoting is that we must *choose* to love the things we genuinely don't love! Chapter 1, Verse 1 of the Book of Lunacism!

PAIRING – THE UNDISCOVERED COUNTRY

There is something important for us to understand about the reason for Sarah and Tom's mismatch—an underlying cause not readily apparent. Normally Sarah is a warm, intelligent, humorous, mild-tempered and thoughtful person. But with Tom she becomes irritable, angry, and argumentative. Although it may seem contradictory, Sarah's personality contains *both* sets of characteristics, sweet and angry. Her friends pull forth her sweet primary traits, whereas Tom pulls forth her secondary, less pleasant traits. Which of her personalities emerges is influenced by the people in her presence. It's all about *pairing*.

Pairing is an artifact of the blending of two people's characteristics—it is what a couple becomes *together*. Mix hydrogen and oxygen molecules in certain pairings and they produce water—peaceful, serene. Under different conditions, it's the Hindenburg. Each partner with whom we are paired brings all of their characteristics to the table—sweet, angry, loving, affectionate, gruff, needy, generous—everything that is possible in the makeup of their personality. When we join with a partner, their characteristics pull certain aspects of our own innate traits to the surface. Sarah needs strength from her partner, but Tom has a tendency to be passive-aggressive. Dealing with his tendencies irritates her and pulls her angry side to the surface. Sarah is not normally angry, but she is with Tom. Exchange Tom for a Magical Match, and her sweet side would come forward instead.

Pairing is a step beyond matching. In traditional relationships, the target is largely about measuring the match: "His characteristics are BMXYZ, hers are ASXYZ. Hey, they're a pretty good match!" But are they really? In terms of measuring by match, a couple's characteristics might be similar, complements, opposites, or even mismatches—and none of those guarantee a successful, long-term relationship. To ensure more successful relationships we need to change the measure; the yardstick must be the *results of pairing. Together* are you angry, sad, or happy? Is the pairing synergistic or does it leave the couple to work on their potholes while the Oranges—all leaning on shovels—circle around and look on? Does pure love deepen and grow, or, like Tom and Sarah, does the pairing continuously pull anger, resentment, or discord into the mix?

Listening to Sarah's story, it was easy for me to see where they had gone wrong. Between the love and the arguments, the good and the bad, the pain and the joy, was an all too common failing. It took me 15 seconds to detect where years of therapy had failed them:

- My diagnosis: They were a poor pairing.
- My advice: *FIND A DIFFERENT PARTNER!*

This pairing did not pull Sarah's best personality traits to the surface. "With a different pairing you won't feel misunderstood, pressured, and angry. Find someone who reveals your best traits and you'll never need another counseling appointment."

Another case solved. I feel like House.

In the end, all the wisdom we've received over the years ends up being true. Not because it is true, but because we *make* it true. When we choose to settle, our relationships require work, effort, and compromise.

But, what would happen if we suddenly decided that these truths were myth? Is it so impossible to believe that you can have a relationship that does not require effort—an effortless relationship? Crazy, isn't it? Maybe…. But who is the lunatic? The man who spends a lifetime learning to love the things that he genuinely doesn't love or the one who believes a better, different relationship exists?

Key Concepts:
- Traditional relationships are outside→in, starting as superficial matches and working their way inward.
- Mismatches are part of the traditional relationship construction that leads to friction, work, and compromise—it's what happens when we settle on a less-than-optimal pairing.
- All of the expertise and advice we understand about relationships is built upon a traditional relationship model.
- Pairing is the result of two people's characteristics mixing together. It is a step beyond matching.

4

THE DISCOVERY OF MIRRORING
THE DISCOVERY OF MIRRORING

"It is wrong to think that love comes from long companionship and persevering courtship. Love is the offspring of spiritual affinity and unless that affinity is created in a moment, it will not be created for years or even generations." - Kahlil Gibran

I am a 20-year veteran of one of those mismatched traditional marriages. I was 20 and far too young when I first walked down the aisle. Even though I imagined a life of domestic splendor and joy spreading out before us, my former wife and I suffered from many of the typical problems that befall those who marry too soon. The ups and downs, the long years of togetherness, grew us into good friends and partners, yet the friction between us led to discord and arguments. I found our marriage largely unfulfilling. In turn, she would probably say that I never really understood her—and that I was absent too long in too many ways.

It comes as no surprise; our relational dysfunction was the result of poor pairing.

Exiting my marriage, I knew that I wanted more. I had long waited for the chance to start again, my determination lying dormant. Determined to have an amazing relationship. Determined to be loved in the way I needed. Determined to have tranquility and harmony. Even though my marriage had failed, I still had hope. I *knew* that I was built for intimate relationship—I *like* being married. So, determined and 20 years out of practice, I waded into the dating pool, wearing my venerable relationship notions as a life preserver. I would meet someone, get to know her, and slowly work towards love. A slow, cautious approach made sense to me. I had never known anything different and it suited my natural tendencies. Yes, a traditional dating process would keep me afloat in these unknown waters.

But I didn't know how to begin. I wasn't much of a barfly and I had a pretty small social circle. I had heard that online dating worked for some people, and it seemed as good a starting place as any. Why not give it a whirl? So I opened a Match.com account, wrote a profile, dropped in a few pictures, and figured that would start the ball rolling in the right direction.

It was pretty exciting, and a little nerve-wracking, to start dating again. Meeting strangers whom I knew little about always began with an awkward slowness, but it (mostly) seemed to improve as the date progressed. I had a handful of dates and met some very nice women. Some dates had a touch of connection and shared enough commonality to make for an enjoyable evening. Some were pretty flat. A few were downright uncomfortable. I saw a couple of women more than once in that traditional-esque date-to-date progression where you hope a connection will grow. The slow and careful traditional progression made for predictable, albeit lackluster, dating.

That trend lasted all of three months—until an evening in January 2008 turned my world right-side up and *profoundly* changed my life. And that's putting it mildly. I had no idea that as I sat down to my first date with Helen that 60 minutes later, I would *know* beyond any doubt that she was a female copy of me—a reflection. Meeting Helen completely exploded all the concepts I had about dating—and it was a total and absolute surprise. From the very *first* moments, our connection was undeniably compelling. We both felt the power of it. *Immediate, palpable gravity*—surreal to the point that it seemed only divine intervention could have played a hand.

WHAT IS THIS THING?

My relationship with Helen launched at breakneck speed. Like a rocket ship, it just seemed to go faster and faster—so fast in fact that it quickly became love, then catapulted into a 28-day engagement. So much for tradition! Everyone thought that I had gone mental. I wanted my friends and family to understand my experience, but describing the connection was impossible. *How could I explain?* There were no words, no language, no analogies. There existed no frame of reference, no guide. Even I didn't fully understand! Regardless, I *knew* it was real.

Everything we know about relationships is from a traditional perspective—and it was so *not* that! How do you describe a connection beyond superlatives? Deeply connected, grounded, peaceful, super-easy, uber-compelling, harmonious, heavenly. She was just like me. We shared the same feelings, we shared similar experiences, and she thought *exactly* the same thoughts I did. She understood me before I ended my sentences. Helen felt precisely the same way. And, unbelievably, our connection just kept growing *stronger*. Describing our connection to others was like trying to explain honesty to a politician. I desperately needed a Rosetta Stone.

Finally, one day, I had an epiphany. There is one relationship wherein two people think, walk, dress, eat, and communicate in the same way. They share an identical set of genes and grow up having the same life experiences. We think of their connection as easy, harmonious, intuitive, rare, and unique. They are reflections of the highest order—Mirrors of each other. And somehow, we seem to innately grok this connection. This was it! Finally! I had found a way to describe our connection.

IDENTICAL TWINS!

Because we've all heard about and seem to understand the connection identical twins share, it provided a reference other people could use to comprehend my experience. That inseparable, deeply bonded, highly compatible, nearly telepathic bond between identical twins was very similar to our bond—only romantic rather than sibling.

But I couldn't stop there. Intrigued by this epiphany, a Google search for *romantic twins* unearthed an artifact that was nothing less than complete, total illumination…

TWIN SOULS

As I searched, I found journals written and read by reincarnationists—people whose religion includes a deep belief in reincarnation. The articles described the ultimate romantic relationship as one in which a single soul is split in two. The two souls are sent forth separately to live multiple lives, learning and growing in each incarnation. Finally, when the souls have learned true, unconditional love, they are reunited in a meeting that reveals a deep, surprising, immediately recognizable connection. Two mirrored souls joined in a romantic coupling that embodies an emotional, physical, and love connection beyond all others—your one perfect Twin.

Twin Souls described *precisely* what I was experiencing and feeling with Helen. Our connection was perfectly described as mirrored souls that had been rejoined. I felt like I had known Helen forever, and she felt as if she had come home. It was surreal, sublime, perfect.

But four months into the relationship, it fell apart. Helen began to withdraw. I did everything I could to bring her back to me, but nothing worked. At the time, I didn't understand what had happened or why—all I knew was that she had pulled away. After all the years I had waited and dreamed for this kind of love to arrive, I thought I had lost my only chance. *My one Twin was gone.* I didn't eat, sleep, or work for nearly a month. I lost 15 pounds from my six-foot frame, finally bottoming out at near 155 pounds. My friends worried. I felt hopeless.

COULD I HAVE MORE THAN ONE?

Despite my heartbreak, I started dating again within a couple of months. I wasn't over Helen yet, but I was determined to get back on the horse. As fate would have it, one evening found me sitting down to another first date. As the conversation turned towards relationships and dating, I found myself talking about Helen, sharing my tale of discovery that started with Identical Twins and led to Twin Souls. I told my date about the experience I'd had and that I *never* expected to feel that type of connection again. Listening to me, she nodded, saying that she had some knowledge of the reincarnationist belief in the rare relationship that stems from meeting your perfect Twin. And then, she told me something that nearly knocked me to the floor.

It can happen more than once!

In her reading, and in her own experience, she had discovered that the ideal reincarnationist relationship was a *conceptual* description. "In reality," she said, "it is possible for it to happen more than once." She assured me that I would find another—and it would be just as strong, just as connected. It would feel just as compelling and alive.

Could it be true? I was still haunted by the loss of Helen. The indelible memory of what we shared was a shadow from which I could not escape. I wanted to feel that same bond and have that same ease, to experience that amazing harmony again. I wanted another copy of me, another reflection—*another Mirror*. No matter how long I had to search, I knew that nothing else would do.

THE FIRST MIRROR PROFILE

Thinking back, I could easily remember those first minutes with Helen. I remembered the depth of our connection, the mirror of my soul and heart that became so clear. I remembered our conversations—every word and place we visited. I remembered how she told me the story of her life—the story of my life—as the magic between us stilled time with enchantment. I remembered the path we traveled our very first night together—entering the restaurant as strangers and leaving as a couple.

Was it really possible? Could that same path be followed a second time to find another Mirror?

In a flash of either brilliance or insanity, I translated the path of our first date into these words:

More than Soul Mates...

*When it comes to online dating, if you want a traditional relationship, write a traditional profile. But if you seek more, a profile based upon the things that you do, the food you like, or the places you've been or want to go will not suffice. I've learned the deepest connections come from **who** you are—that little part inside that you think no one will ever understand. When someone does understand it, the connection that happens is deep and immediate, calm and peaceful. You feel like you've known that person forever. It's like the feeling of coming home.*

If the following describes you, we likely share something incredible.

Do you believe every breath in life is a gift?

In romance: Do you follow your heart? Is it easy, and do you often write or speak your feelings and emotions? Can you write a deep love letter? Are you in your heart more than in your head?

Do you truly believe that the most important things in life are the people you love? Are you of the mind that in the grand scheme, love and life lend perspective to everything else?

Do you believe in the power of forgiveness? You don't keep score. You forgive and forget.

Would you prefer to speak of alternatives rather than fight? Do you believe that anger is largely unnecessary?

Do you often put yourself in the other person's shoes and see their perspective?

Are you naturally introspective? In any problem, do you tend to look inside?

Are you able to see your contribution to the issue, even if it is very small?

Are you outgoing, happy, and gregarious? Has that been a source of jealousy with previous partners?

Are you kind and caring? Somewhere inside do you feel that the meek may indeed inherit the earth? Do you believe that an act of kindness, no matter how small, is never wasted?

Are you innately empathetic? Do you find joy in supporting your partner?

Does "Live, Forgive, Laugh, Learn, Love" resonate with you?

Do you tend to find the positive side?

Do you believe in romantic love? Do you believe there is passion and beauty in life? Are you a feminine woman who longs to be treated like a lady?

Do you believe that deeply-connected loving relationships exist? Do you seek an intimate relationship—both physical and mental? Can passion overtake you at any moment?

Are you innately faithful, honest, and compassionate? Are you a one man woman? Is the one-night stand a foreign concept?

Have your previous partners thought you too sensitive? Are you a tender, feeling person? Does your touch sometimes convey more than words?

Do you seek a best friend, as well as a companion? Do you believe there are a few men who are built differently than the rest? (I guess one look at this profile should answer that question. Ha!) Is your life and heart prepared for an amazing relationship?

Are you at a place in your life where you believe it's your turn—a time to begin to concentrate on you and that special one?

Do you believe in loving fully? Do you understand, and have you given, unconditional love? Was it returned? Do you have a tendency to be unguarded and vulnerable?

As you read this, do you feel that there is a place inside of you that's been touched? Do you see yourself in the mirror created by these words?

If the above deeply resonates within you, then you understand who I am inside. You and I likely share the rarest of connections. We might be more than soul mates.

I don't have to invite you to email me...you've already decided....

I am passionately committed to finding that one partner for a deeply connected, monogamous, long-term relationship filled with fun, joy, and harmony.

When I finished, I posted it as my new Match.com profile.

In clicking that final Submit button, I had no idea that I was about to embark on a three-year exploration of Mirrors. In that time, my Mirror Profile would trek across Match.com, eHarmony, Chemistry, Yahoo Personals, and Plenty-of-Fish, drawing replies from near and far in an odyssey that would teach me more about deep love, matching, profiling, and even heartbreak, than I had ever imagined. I had no idea how many despondent daters would tell me stories of endless searching without finding true love. In return, I would share tales of my Mirror dating, insisting that it was possible to have truly inspiring connections with some *90%* of all dates.

As for me, it would take three short years, just 30 first dates, to define a different type of relationship. Even more astounding, my experience would prove you *can* bottle lightning.

It was…

   …a new path,

      a predictable path,

         a reproducible path.

I had discovered *the Mirror path…*

What had started as an act of desperation became The Mirror Effect.

Key Concepts

- Meeting someone just like you, a Mirror, is a sudden, profound experience.
- Describing the connection Mirrors share is nearly impossible. The only real way to understand it is to experience it yourself.
- The relationship between Mirrors is like that of Identical Twins or Twin Souls

Mirror Effect Law

- You have many Mirrors.

5

MY MAGICAL MATCH

"I have loved to the point of madness;
That which is called madness, That which to me,
Is the only sensible way to love."
–Françoise Sagan

In July 2008, I met Judy for the first time. I was in Paris, still in some shock over losing Helen. I had seen Judy's profile on Match.com. *Not for the Faint of Heart* was her headline to a profile that spoke of a heart seeking deep, intimate love. Of all the profiles I read, I found hers uniquely appealing. We had emailed back and forth a couple of times, but I was still not in the best space for dating.

July 2, 2008

Hi from Paris, Judy,
The timing isn't just right now, but you never know. Maybe it will bring us back to share a dance in the future.

Thanks again for emailing with me. I wish you all the best in finding that special someone.

Troy

But Paris worked its magic, and despite my initial response, I decided to meet Judy. Besides, her profile *was* intriguing; maybe there was something there. Little did I know at the time how our dance would weave its way through Peter Frampton, Paris in July, two years and two first dates...and ultimately to my Magical Match.

Ten days later, on a warm California evening, Judy and I met at an Italian restaurant. We spent hours talking about relationships and love, work and all the little things that two people—even those who despise small talk—converse about. Afterwards, we walked downtown. In amongst the people and the warm July night, we walked side by side getting to know each other. At some point I reached for her hand. She donned a cute shy look that comes from a little girl place and softly said, "I think I'm supposed to be coy right now," as she gently moved her hand away. We stopped in Starbucks, talked some more and made plans to meet the following Tuesday to see Peter Frampton at the Mountain Winery.

The plan called for a picnic dinner before the concert. The picnic was Judy's idea and she went out of her way to make something special. That day also saw me waiting for my new sports car to be delivered. The delivery guy was running hours late, and so were we for our concert picnic. But the car finally arrived and five minutes later I was off to pick up Judy.

Frampton really rocked the evening, and so did Judy. Wine, great music, and Judy dancing in the aisles under the evening stars. A ripping cover of "While My Guitar Gently Weeps" ended the evening with a signature Frampton power riff that brought the house down. On the way home, a stop for midnight crepes caught us dancing in the restaurant as we ended our second date on a high note.

At that time, Judy was also dating someone else. They had only been on a few more dates than we had. Emerging from Helen, I was just beginning the journey into Mirroring and wasn't sure Judy was it. We hadn't started off with quite the same immediate connection and gravity I'd shared with Helen, which left me unsure. There was certainly some gravity with Judy, but it wasn't nearly as strong. I was open about how I felt with Judy, and she responded by letting me know that she liked me, but that she wasn't the type to be anyone's number 2—and she didn't date men on the rebound.

So she chose to continue seeing John, the other man she had been dating. And so after three wonderful dates, our dance ended. I was very sad about her going.

Occasionally, I would drive through Judy's neighborhood and think about her. The time we spent together had been really enjoyable, but the connection wasn't incredibly strong. I didn't really ponder why. It was simply a reflection of the pairing at the time.

Turning the clock forward to July 2010, as I readied for my annual trip to Paris, I was pleasantly surprised to receive an email from Judy. She had tickets to see Peter Frampton again and asked me to come along. She was still involved with John, but they were beginning to see other people. Since I was planning to be overseas at the time of the concert, I declined. Besides, Judy's closet was still full with another man's clothes. How can you have room for finding the love of your life if there's no room in your closet?

Even though I didn't go to the concert, Judy and I decided to have dinner to catch up. In the course of making arrangements, Judy sent me an email for a personal growth workshop she was planning to attend. And she asked, "Does this type of event interest you?"

I could have answered simply, but instead I used her question to share with her on a much more open, transparent basis:

From: Troy Pummill
Sent: Thursday, July 15, 2010 3:59 PM
To: 'Judy Day'
Subject: RE: A Summer Personal Growth Workout!!

Judy,

(I'm smiling here) Wanting to speak for myself, and it's also impossible to overlook what seems pretty obvious from your emails.

I believe it's important to acknowledge truths, even as they may be couched within. It seems as if we're both interested in more than just friends getting together; there seems to be facets of exploring.

I have thoughts about that (that are mostly good)—happy to share those when we meet, if you're interested.

More to your question, I don't spend time working on myself in the ways that I know you do. My spirituality, my depth, is more organic. With the right match, the right heart and soul—I'm quite deep and emotionally available, sensitive, compassionate, and loving, especially for a male. For me, love and touch are essential. So is romance. I've been told that I have a high EQ. My problem has (mostly) been finding a partner that is ready to meet me in the deep canyon that is my heart and soul. In those deep places, I lay there waiting—open, yearning—for a woman whose heart is as deep as mine. Truly amazing, deep, wonderful, joyous, connected intimacy follows, in every way....

Long, and genuine, answer to your question. lol

Does that help?

For what does your heart yearn, Judy?

From: Judy Day
Sent: Friday, July 16, 2010 10:41 AM
To: 'Troy Pummill'
Subject: RE: A Summer Personal Growth Workout!

What a great email and I am laughing out loud. I suppose I am pretty transparent.

Yes, I am oriented to meeting you with an exploring mind, not only just catching up.

Just so you know I did "break up" with John about 10 days ago. And we still have a friendship and work relationship. It will go through a lot of changes in the next few months I am sure. And I know I need time to process it all and transition.

I love the question—what does your heart yearn for? I have been pondering that recently. If you would like I'll let you know what I have so far on Saturday.

From: Troy Pummill
Sent: Friday, July 16, 2010 2:27 PM
To: 'Judy Day'
Subject: RE: A Summer Personal Growth Workout!

You've got me laughing. Transparency is a gift, even though many side to the contrary. There are gifts all around us, if we but have eyes to see them.

Thanks for sharing about John; certainly does provide some clarity and understanding. Know that I am sensitive to your ending, and also strongly believe that things come in the time they are meant to be. If it is our time, then the path will be illuminated by our uniqueness regardless of where we are at this very moment. Two year cycles are a long time, even in online dating parlance....lol!

Since we are officially exploring (lol...how funny is that?), I think it's a probably a good idea to start at the beginning.

This is my profile. It has been an excellent tool in finding those who match me well. Would you be willing to have a read?

I'd love to know your reaction to it. Is it a mirror for you? Do you see yourself in it? Mildly resonates? Goosebumps? Nausea?

Genuinely looking forward to tomorrow and hearing your heart's yearnings. I will be listening...

From: Judy Day
Sent: Friday, July 16, 2010 5:17 PM
To: 'Troy Pummill'
Subject: Your Profile

I love the openness and vulnerability of your profile. I also love that you are really clear on what you want. The fact that you are looking for a deep committed relationship and willing to work on it is extremely attractive. And it is amazing that with just these two qualities you are not bombarded (or maybe you are) with women. After all this is what most women say they want. And even as I write that, I know better.

I believe the type of relationship you are talking about is both possible and rare. I also believe that before being able to be in such a connection you need to know yourself very well and be able to be present and available. And you have to actually want it enough to make it a priority and to surrender to it.

So yes, your profile resonates with me and scares me. No hint of nausea, but a lot of curiosity. To be honest I was in bed last night asking myself, "If I were on my deathbed and declared that my life had not been a total success, where would I have fallen short?" Here is what I came up with:

I never had a long lasting, loving, fun, committed relationship with a man who I surrendered into love with. A relationship where we created our best life according to what was true and real and alive within us.

I never fully became and expressed my full capacity for compassion, peace, and love.

These were the two biggest so I will leave it here.

From: Troy Pummill
Sent: Sat 7/17/2010 10:51 AM
To: 'Judy Day'
Subject: Good morning!

Thank you so much for being open, honest, and vulnerable. Those are qualities I both cherish and encourage—they are essential, and the essence, of the one I seek. This is why my profile exists; to be a mirror, and no, it absolutely does not provide a reflection for the masses.

Again, your insights, or maybe intuition, serve you well—you clearly understand what it takes to have a deep relationship. In my experience, that's very rare. I'm drawn to your clarity of thought and ability to articulate. Very attractive indeed…

Judy, thank you so much for being open to share these parts of you. Would it surprise you to hear that I already understood this about you? I do.

More than you yet know, you are here, in this time and place, for a reason.

Whether it is just a single evening, or much longer…

t

WHAT A DIFFERENCE TWO YEARS MAKES

I was nervous and unsure when Judy opened the door to her home at the beginning of our "second" first date. Two years ago, there had definitely been a shared pull, but the timing hadn't been right. I'd been on the rebound and not really available; she was already involved with someone else. I was hopeful, but unsure about what might happen this time.

A quiet Italian restaurant near the ocean was the setting for our rediscovery. Talk started small and then deepened. We spoke of relationships and where we had been in the last two years. This time, the energy was different between us. Our reflection was clear and the connection incredibly strong. Judy revealed a different part of herself, a deeper place. Where before she had been more guarded and protected, this time she came from her soul. Rather than purposely being coy, she was open and authentic. Her longing for deep connection, emotion, and love resonated strongly for me. Once again, I had that familiar feeling—as if I had known her all my life. Instead of the usual tentativeness that comes with first dates, there was a peaceful ease. Instead of a maybe, there was a *knowing, a deep recognition that the woman in front of me was a Mirror.*

And because she was my Mirror—open and vulnerable—something happened to both of us that night that had never happened before on a first date—not even with Helen. During the evening, both of us started to *fall in love.* And we've been in love every moment since.

We are more than soul mates. We are a Magical Match.

Troy, my love,

For the first 15 plus years of my life, I was under the impression that I was unlovable, somehow different than others who seemed to have love and heartfelt connection with family and friends. I fell short somewhere. Because I never felt this for myself I could only attribute it to something missing or wrong with me. The pain was so great in my early years that I closed my heart up to protect it and built a big strong wall between the inner me and the outside world. I didn't realize that by doing this I was locking myself away.

It took me into my late twenties before I realized that I had characteristics that some thought special, or could even be considered exceptional in their combination. But to open my heart was still a long road for me. I knew I cried easily and was very sensitive, but I had so fiercely protected that part of myself for so many years that I found it difficult to open to it. Actually I didn't know how.

Then I met you. From our second first date I knew I loved you. Your being seemed to be a part of mine. I quickly became aware of and felt the river that runs through and between us. It is the river of life and it is obvious that our souls travel the same river, that our hearts connect here. This river is on this plane and at the same time on another plane, timeless and ethereal.

Your love allows me to be more myself than I have ever been. For the first time, I see a life with a man I choose to love rather than a promise or a hope of what may be but never comes to pass. Your love is an immense energy and power that has the ability to ground me and connect me to myself and to your heart. It is the beauty in my life, the foundation for all that we will create together. With you, my energy rises, my excitement for life increases, my commitment to live my own potential is nurtured. I see that from this love we can create great things. Life changing things. For ourselves and others.

I knew you were my husband one day in bed—just like when you open your eyes in the dark at 5 am you know the sun will banish the dark and light will shine on you by 8. I know this relationship is mine. I've claimed it and will not let it go. I will nurture it and cherish it always.

I feel like the luckiest woman in the world. You are the one I have been waiting for, the one I can travel into the deepest depths of my heart and soul, can open up into places I have never visited before, and land safely in love.

I commit to loving you and living our lives together in the fullness of each moment. To encourage each other to do what makes us most happy and alive. To nurture our love as my primary commitment and accept your heart as a gift I get to open each day.

I now have the completing, missing piece of my life. It is you. You have the keys to my heart, the keys to unlock my love. You are the man with whom I commit to build the most joyous, deep, intimate love and life with that transcends this material plane and lets me fly on its wings. I have come home into you.

I love you and am yours

-Judy (written October 5, 2010)

THE ROAD TO FINDING YOUR MAGICAL MATCH

The story of our Magical Match is just that—magical. Amazingly romantic, stirring and, to some, mysterious. It is all those things and much more—and it is not by accident. Meeting and falling in love with Judy was not some incredibly rare alignment of planets, magnetization, fate, nor any other quasi-mystical causality. Our relationship was *engineered*—created by my experience in harnessing the power of the Mirror Effect.

Magical relationships, like the one that Judy and I share, have always existed. Those fortunate few who happened to be in the right place at the right time could be struck by lightning and receive the gift of the unparalleled relationship.

With the Mirror Effect, lightning is no longer a rarity of circumstance. Lightning can be engineered: created, filtered, selected, and bottled.

And it can be yours. All you need to do is understand the Mirror Effect and its elements.

Key Concepts

- The relationship between Mirrors is unlike any other relationship.
- There is a clear, recognizable pathway to finding a Mirror. Lightning can be bottled.
- When you meet your Mirror, it is perfectly natural to quickly fall deeply in love.
- Once you understand the concept of Mirroring and learn the steps to finding your Magical Match you, too, can take advantage of the Mirror Effect.

Mirror Effect Law

- You don't choose the relationship; the relationship chooses you.

6

UNDERSTANDING
THE MIRROR EFFECT

"Your task is not to seek for love, but merely to seek and find all the barriers within yourself that you have built against it."–Rumi

In order to find your Magical Match, you must first thoroughly understand the concepts, elements, and experience of all things Mirror:

- The definitions of Mirrors and The Mirror Effect
- The components of The Mirror Effect
- The blueprint for a Mirror relationship

After a lifetime learning the traditional, we invite you to discard the old ways in order to discover a different type of relationship. So forget everything you've ever learned about relationships and prepare to take a step into a world both magical *and* tangible.

WHAT ARE MIRRORS?

A Mirror is someone *just* like you. The deepest needs, wants, desires, feelings, understandings, beliefs—everything critical to a relationship—is shared. Every aspect below the surface layer is the same. Mirrors embody identical mentality, spirituality, emotionality, life perspectives, sexuality, ethics, and sense of humor. Mirrors even share similar life situations, predilections, views on relationships, politics, education, and so much more.

Here's what one woman said about meeting her Mirror:

"After ending a twenty-eight year marriage, I met a man online who captivated my soul. Despite the fact that he was ten years younger, we shared a magical connection that transcended age and time itself. Quickly we found ourselves whisked into the vortex of passionate love and the hints of ecstatic union. I had never known this type of intensity before—one that mirrored my own essence so profoundly. After knowing him for just three weeks, he invited me to join him on a three-week business trip. Those three weeks felt more like three months. There was something mysteriously known and familiar about him and the synergy between us. It was almost as if I was able to reach back through the vale of time and remember a soul pact we had made long ago."

Mirrors are two people who are so extremely alike in sharing a single heart, mind, and soul that it feels as though each is looking into a mirror reflection of the other.

WHAT IS THE MIRROR EFFECT?

The Mirror Effect is the principle that defines all the resulting relationship characteristics shared by Mirrors. *It describes, defines, and explains the extraordinary Mirror pairing.*

WHAT IS A MAGICAL MATCH?

A Magical Match is someone with whom you share the ultimate pairing of peace, harmony, and an incredibly deep love bond. You and your Magical Match complete each other, have mind-blowing chemistry, and an effortless relationship.

Why do we call it a Magical Match? It's because that's what it feels like.

You will likely meet several Mirrors along your journey, but only one of those can be your Magical Match.

A Magical Match is the Mirror you select as a life partner.

WHAT ARE THE MIRROR EFFECT ELEMENTS?

Why does Mirror dating feel the way it does? How can it be possible to *know* in the time it takes to quaff a bottle of Napa Cabernet? Why is the experience of this relationship so different?

It's different because when you are with a Mirror, the *resulting* elements are very different than those of a traditional relationship; *The Mirror Effect produces a distinctive set of characteristics that define a Mirror relationship.*

By coming to understand each of these elements you will be able to understand and recognize when you've met a Mirror. These elements are:

- Communication
- Chemistry
- Compatibility
- Similar Life Experiences
- Profound Connection
- Accelerated Time
- The Knowing
- The Feeling
- The Peace

Element #1 – Communication

Like identical twins, *Mirrors share an uncanny level of communication.* For Mirrors, words are often unnecessary. Whereas most couples require varying levels of explanation to achieve an understanding, Mirrors often complete each other's sentences or thoughts. When one partner is at a loss for words to describe an emotion, the other will supply the *perfect* articulation.

It goes *beyond* just being able to arrive at the same conclusion. Mirrors can often predict where their partner is going with a thought or within a conversation. Even more compelling is the fact that when you're in a Mirror relationship, you can *predict* what your Mirror will say or do just by thinking about how you would handle the same situation.

Element #2 – Chemistry

Mirror chemistry is nothing less than incredible. Whether it be conversational, intellectual, chemical, physical appearance, or some other type of chemistry, the spark between Mirrors is impossible to ignore, and the sexual energy is undeniable. Contrary to simple lust or infatuation, Mirrors share a physical bond as an outpouring of a soul connection. Instead of being driven by hormones, it's a deep flowing river of love.

Element #3 – Compatibility

Extreme compatibility is a Mirror hallmark. Neat or messy, quiet or talkative, head or heart, frugal or extravagant, introvert or extrovert, toilet roll over the top or toilet roll under the bottom, being together is easy. Mirrored couples coexist without friction or adjustment.

Element #4 – Similar Life Experiences

Part of the unique connection shared by Mirrors comes from *sharing similar life paths.* Work, family, relationships, pain, brokenness, successes—whatever it is—is shared. Parallel life paths lead to an empathic connection, the feeling that "*finally* someone understands who I am and what I've been through."

Element #5 – Profound Connection

Mirroring at this level creates an *instant* soul connection, a bond that surpasses all other bonds. Love forms at impossible speeds.

Element #6 – Accelerated Time

Every Mirror relationship experiences *accelerated time.* For Mirrors, even though it's only been a week, you *feel* like you've known each other a month. A month feels like three, three months feel like a year, six months feel like forever. In the strongest Mirrors, there is no feeling of time whatsoever—it's as though you've always known each other.

Instead of spending years coming to know our partner's depths, Mirrors spend time filling in pieces of a life that has always been shared, but never actually lived together. Although you might think that this progression would feel surreal—and it does a little—it usually feels more natural than not.

In the end, Mirror relationships achieve in minutes what decades-long relationships only begin to approach.

Element #7 – The Knowing

From the first date, there is a *knowing*, an innate realization that something special is happening. It just feels obvious—like it was meant to be. It seems impossible, but you just know that it is real. It is almost a feeling of divine intervention.

Element #8 – The Feeling

A unique Mirror Effect characteristic is the feeling of *knowing this person forever* or *the feeling of coming home*. The Feeling results from the blending of all the other Mirror Effect elements, but nevertheless, The Feeling is a distinct element unto itself.

Element #9 – The Peace

Deeply seated, almost ethereal, there is a peace and harmony around your pairing.

The first Mirror encounter is simultaneously beautiful and daunting. Understanding the various elements[1] makes the experience less confusing—and the less confusion there is in dating the better!

---

[1] The usual relationship traits you're familiar with (spirituality, attraction, sexuality, mentality, etc.) are all encompassed within the Mirror Effect Elements.

A NEW DIRECTION IN RELATIONSHIPS

Mirror relationships are built from the inside→out: meeting first at the soul. Due to this different blueprint, the construction will be very different than your previous experiences. Time to bulldoze dilapidated ideas! Let's begin to frame a new union based upon what the Mirror Effect shows us about:

- the different stages of Mirror relationships
- the new guidelines for Mirror relationships
- the new challenges brought by Mirror relationships
- the myths exposed by Mirror relationships

Your ideals and expectations are about to be challenged. *Don't* hang on to your hats!

The Radically Different Stages of the Mirror Relationship

A traditional relationship has a progression that is endemic to its outside→in pattern. The reason traditional dating proceeds slowly is that exploration begins from a superficial connection. The need for a lengthy courtship is driven by the amount of time required to discover the character of your partner's heart and soul.

If, however, we begin with a soul connection and build from the inside→out, the resulting relationship stages are quite different:

Stage #1 – The Epiphany

The date begins with the sudden realization that you already *know* this person. The typical interview questions feel unnecessary as you look into your date's eyes and see yourself.

The Epiphany mingles amazement with incredulity. There is also very little question—The Knowing, The Feeling, and The Peace are present. The Mirror Effect creates inescapable gravity that easily and so calmly overruns every sense that might scream *impossible*.

Instead of spending the typical weeks trying to ascertain if you should continue dating, the relationship simply begins—and continues with a pace of discovery that approaches nearly instantaneous.

In essence, the relationship chooses you.

You've just skipped over "traditional dating."

Stage #2 – Relationship

All of the Mirror Effect elements are synergized, giving your relationship wings with which to fly. Your beloved consumes your every thought and moment. Falling deeply in love occurs in less than a month. Discussion of marriage, moving in together, and commitment tend to happen very quickly, so this stage can be very short. Because of the speed of the relationship, any weaknesses or mismatches are already beginning to surface.

Stage #3 – Engagement

In a prototypical traditional relationship, engagement occurs around the one-year mark. Due to accelerated time, that same "it's time for engagement" feeling occurs *much* sooner in a Mirror relationship. Even though it is often too soon to know if the relationship will actually result in commitment, engagement *feels* right.

It's an intermixing of an old idea with the realities of a new relationship paradigm. Mirror engagement is more a recognition of the *willingness* to surrender to the connection. It is a time to go deeper and ensure there aren't any hidden mismatches—to discover if your Mirror is indeed your Magical Match.

This stage typically lasts less than a year, sometimes just a few months.

Unlike traditional engagement, it's better to think of Mirror engagement as a willingness to surrender to Connection rather than an actual promise to marry.

Stage #4 – Commitment

Marriage and/or living together is a blissful state for Magical Matches. A lifetime of easy happiness and joy awaits those who successfully reach the end of the Mirroring Process.

We strongly suggest that you make no permanent commitment (don't get married, leave your job, sell your house, or move to another country) before reaching six months in the relationship. The deep love and connection might make this suggestion seem silly, but it is for the better.

Observe how the Mirror relationship moves simply, progressively forward. No twists, no unnatural acts, while the traditional relationship is scattered, elongated, and complicated:

- Is there enough interest to have a second date?
- Are there enough commonalities to move forward to exclusivity?
- Am I going to be able to fall in love and get to engagement?

So many questions. And that's just the beginning of the relationship!

New Relationship, New Guidelines

In Mirror dating, you can dispense with traditional ideals and guidelines: Should I email him? Wait two days before calling? Never kiss on the first date? All of these games that we are taught or somehow learn only make things worse; they feed mistrust, reinforce walls, and block potential. They result in wasted time and effort.

There are maxims specific to Mirror relationships. Authenticity, openness, balance, ease—these are the new bylaws. Take heed. These new guiding commandments are important for both finding and keeping you on the path to your Magical Match:

Guideline #1 – Transparency

Transparency is the currency of connection in the Mirror Effect. Walls and lack of authenticity are barriers to discovery. Conversely, openness and transparency allow a pure, unfiltered reflection so that you can see the depth and makeup of the reflection. The more open you are, the more the Mirror Effect can come into play. So, prepare to drop your force fields and lean in!

Guideline #2 – The Tango

The Tango is sublimely analogous to a relationship; it is *the* dance for the Mirror relationship paradigm. The tango is hot, sexy, intimate! It flows like two lovers in passion's heat, locked together as they move perfectly in unison. A red rose between the teeth, the little black dress, high heels, a fragrance floating on air as *Por Una Cabeza* meets each step in a tempo only lovers feel.

The Tango is also quite technical. There is a progression of steps to be learned and practiced. Rules of the dance guide what should be done, and when. Of all the elements that give the tango its stunning and sharp beauty, the *frame* is crucial. A solid frame, the way in which the dancers hold each other, creates the foundation for a perfect tango. The dancer's frame creates a distinct space between their bodies. As they move around the dance floor, this space moves with them. As one partner moves forward, he moves into the place where the space was, pushing his partner backwards. The couple alternatively moves backward and forward, thus sharing the space, creating balance in the dance.

In the same way as a dance, your actions affect the balance of a relationship. When your partner says "I love you," she is pushing forward and leading the dance. As she has taken the lead, your response, 'I love you, too,' holds the frame and maintains the space as she advances. Your response provides something for her to push into—a firmness that reflects trust and strength in your coupling.

But providing a strong, responsive frame is only part of maintaining balance in the dance. If she is always the initiator, always leading, then she is constantly pressing into the space. A constant stream of initiation by one partner—saying "I love you", sending text messages, emails, IMs, flowers, cards, kissing, hugging, just touching—can make it feel like there is no space for the other to initiate. Without the opportunity to lead, growth is suffocated and love stifled. If one partner is always leading then the other partner will eventually tire, lose the frame and destroy the symmetry of the dance, as well as of the relationship.

Balance is everything in a Magical Match relationship. You must both lead and follow to have a balanced relationship. Be mindful of your Tango! Meet your partner's steps and hold a solid frame. Don't lean in too much, but don't lean out too much either.

> "But let there be spaces in your togetherness and let the winds of the heavens dance between you. Love one another but make not a bond of love: let it rather be a moving sea between the shores of your souls." —Kahlil Gibran, *The Prophet*

Guideline #3 – Follow the Connection

When you find a Mirror connection, follow it. That is not to say follow it blindly—you must be mindful of all you learn about Mirroring and the Mirroring Process.

A few Mirror Effect Laws are also important guidelines for the relationship itself:

- **If It's Work, It's Wrong**
  This is the #1 Mirror Effect Law. *The **work** in relationships is in direct proportion to the level of mismatches.* The greater the mismatches in a pairing, the more effort is required to keep the relationship alive.

  If you're "working" at a relationship, it's not a Mirror relationship. If there is a gnawing discomfort, then there is something wrong. Even if you're just feeling uneasy about a particular aspect, something that just doesn't quite jibe, then it's probably a near miss—a Mirror who isn't your Magical Match.

- **Sometimes Love is Not Enough**
  This is another of the Mirror relationship Laws that is also a guideline. Although meeting a Mirror is a life-changing, mind-blowing experience, life does not always mimic a Harlequin romance. Cinderella is not going to leave a slipper for you to find at the Mirror Matching Ball. Prince Charming is not going to appear at your portal (web or otherwise), knock down the door, and carry you off into the sunset.

  In the real world, especially in the Mirror Effect realm, love is sometimes not enough. The problem comes when we connect deeply at the soul and then believe that the deepest love will conquer all. It doesn't.

  Why not, you ask? How could a connection this profound not be right?

  Here's a simple example. You meet a Mirror and feel the ultimate connection, yet that Mirror is already in a committed relationship, unable to separate. Or maybe the Mirror you meet, like Helen, is so injured by life that, even in the light of the Mirror love, she cannot get past her walls of mistrust and pain.

  Love will find a way is a wonderful, romantic notion. And yes, love is a powerful, palpable life force, but logistics, brokenness, mismatches, money, distance, and countless other obstacles can block love's path.

  The saving grace is that we have more than one Mirror. Love *will* find a way, just with a different Mirror.

- **Everything is Opposite**
  And the last guideline to consider is that compared to traditional relationships, almost everything in the Mirror relationship is the opposite:

- Traditional is outside→in. Mirror is inside→out.
- Traditional is slow. Mirror is fast.
- Traditional dating is loosely defined. Mirror is methodically stepped.
- Traditional is tenuous and unsure. Mirror is connected, solid , assured, obvious.
- Traditional dating diminishes your confidence. Mirror dating builds confidence.
- Traditional is about what to do to be a better dater. Mirror is about being yourself—completely.
- Traditional is about marketing. Mirror is about filtering.
- Traditional is love-before-match. Mirror is match-before-love.
- Traditional is about building connection. Mirror is about a connection that already exists.

New matching game, new matching guidelines. The Mirror Effect changes how we approach dating—and how we execute that approach is critically important to our success. Fortunately, like everything Mirror, the ideals are simple, clearly cut, and provide an excellent framework to keep you on the path.

New Challenges

Every new paradigm presents new challenges. Just like traditional relationships, Mirror relationships have challenges—it's just that the challenges are different. Being aware of these challenges will assist you in adapting and responding in a way that will keep your Mirror Relationship on track:

Challenge #1 – Pressure

Rather than a traditional relationship Crock-Pot, one that slowly simmers the mismatches into the stew, Mirror Relationships are a pressure cooker. The element of accelerated time compacts years of a relationship into weeks and months, creating a pressure only a highly bonded, deeply connected relationship can withstand.

Even though new Mirror Relationships are incredibly strong and connected, they are also fresh and fragile. This is one of the many paradoxes of the Mirror Effect. Under this pressure, *there is a higher level of insecurity because the stakes, pressure, and emotions are so much higher.* Little things get amplified. A simple small, transitory relationship air pocket can feel like freefall—and can trigger a *bolting* instinct that stems from the vulnerability of sharing such a deep connection.

Even given this heightened state, the accelerated pace of the relationship is a gift. The pressure forces real and transitory problems to the surface and allows Mirrors to see very quickly what doesn't work in a pairing. If there is a true weakness in the pairing, the pressure will likely cause the relationship to naturally self-destruct. This is one of the self-correcting facets of the Mirror Effect.

The challenge, and wisdom, is just to let it all happen as it naturally should. These relationships are peaceful and easy when you let them flow rather than allowing the thoughts in your head get in the way. Rather than follow the instinct to bolt, initiate an open discussion when a situation arises. Just be yourself. Be authentic in whatever you are feeling, speak whatever thoughts you have, do whatever comes naturally to you. When you're with a Mirror, doing these things will strengthen everything about the relationship and provide clear evidence that you are indeed right where you are supposed to be.

Challenge #2 – The Death Spiral

Relationships often reach a place where one partner encounters some problem or issue that unbalances the Tango. Prevailing wisdom says to give space and time to your partner. *I'm going to step back for a moment while you figure this out.*

In fact, this is the opening maneuver in the Death Spiral.

The Death Spiral occurs when one, or both, of the partners are not strong within the relationship. A Death Spiral starts when Jade backs away because she feels Stephan has taken the smallest step backwards. Feeling Jade moving away, Stephan backs away. A vicious cycle ensues until the Tango is broken and the couple is no longer standing on the dance floor. The relationship dies.

Tragically, Stephan might not have actually backed up at all. It could all have been Jade's imagination. A perfectly good relationship might have Death Spiraled because of misinterpretation and miscommunication.

Here's an example. After falling in love in a single evening, I sent Judy the following email the next day:

My dearest Judy,

I'm almost never without words, but I find myself just that—speechless. I feel such a deep connection and likeness—a comfort and harmony and peace with you. How rare and wonderful it is to experience those things, and with a woman who is truly beautiful—inside and out.

If I'm honest, I miss you. There were too few precious seconds; I wasn't yet ready to leave you.

I am thankful to you for being brave enough to search me out; for your warmth, willingness, and openness; for nurturing me this morning with breakfast; and for sharing our first moments of passion and tenderness. I am so incredibly blessed.

My hand is upon your heart until next we meet...

t

Her reply to that email began like this:

Speechless sums it up perfectly.

On a practical level—did I happen to leave my sunglasses in your car? I am a bit lost without them.

I am not just speechless but kind of in shock to be honest.

This certainly wasn't the response I expected after the supernatural experience of discovering we were Mirrors the night before. Somehow the brain doesn't process, *"Speechless, do you have my sunglasses?"* as *"I'm falling in love with you in the most amazing way I've ever known or thought possible!"* Hmmmm…

At that moment, it would have been completely natural for me to fall into fear *and to risk her feeling me take that step back.* If I had done so, it could have very easily initiated a Death Spiral. Instead I sent this:

> I so get your shock—understandable and normal. I stand here, unwavering, as you experience. Wherever you are, I will be there to hold you, listen, and honor your heart's path.

I held a perfect Tango, neither pushing in nor leaning out. Two days later, that perfect Tango was rewarded with a partner who firmed up her framing and stepped solidly into the dance.

> The shock has subsided and I am left happily looking forward to being with you again.
> I can feel you in my mind and in my body as I walk through the house.

Your strength in a steady stance creates a warm, compelling invitation for your Mirror to keep dancing. Ignore the urge to give space. When your partner wavers, gets scared, or panics, continue to stand on the dance floor:

- Hold your partner in the perfect Tango—perfect frame, perfect balance.
- Open the communication lines if your partner begins to pull away.
- Don't lean in too hard. Continue to say "I love you," but no more or less than normal.

Just keep dancing while holding your partner's eyes. Doing so will draw her back into the tango, quickly reestablishing critical balance.

Challenge #3 – Don't Try to Control the Relationship

The speed of the relationship can be daunting. It's like you're being swept off your feet and carried away in a flash flood, leaving you with no control of the relationship's speed or direction.

Our traditional indoctrination tells us that nothing is supposed to move this quickly, so the tendency is to try and control the pace and course. This is a mistake. Like any law of nature or science, if you change the conditions, the law may cease to function.

For instance, if the moment is right to kiss and you don't, then your connection may be weakened. If you're in love and don't say so because traditionally it's too early, then the next step in the Mirror relationship may not develop naturally.

Attempting to control a Mirror relationship may lead to a failure in the Mirror Effect and inadvertently kill a Magical Match. The best advice is to let the relationship develop naturally, whatever and however that is.

Challenge #4 – Decision vs. Discovery

Due to accelerated time, discovery of mismatches will not occur *before* the formation of the relationship. The natural progression for a Mirror relationship can lead to a decision (commitment, cohabitation, engagement, marriage, relocation) within weeks, yet the typical timing for discovery is between 8 weeks and 4 months. You do the math: Almost invariably, any issues between Mirrors surface *after* the relationship is already well under way.

Challenge #5 – Risk vs. Reward

Risk and reward are equal brothers—one cannot exist without the other. As a Magical Match is the ultimate relationship, the ultimate reward, there must be an equal, corresponding risk.

It's like climbing Everest—the ultimate climb comes with the greatest risks. As we climb, our partner may become injured. He may hit the wall and be unable to climb further. She may slip and fall off the mountain. Just as in mountaineering, there are many hazards on the way to love's summit.

The odds are that you will likely experience more than one Mirror relationship before you find your Magical Match. It hurts like hell to lose one of these relationships. It can be devastating.

Yet, each Mirror relationship is amazingly beautiful and can enable us to grow. When we learn that it is possible to have a second chance, we grow stronger. And so it goes; growing stronger with each relationship until we realize that we have, quite by accident, learned to climb and fall. We learn to love without need or extreme attachment, and in doing so it becomes possible to savor the love in each relationship for however long it lasts.

Remember, no one reaches the pinnacle without risk. Risk is inherent in love. As you will learn, openness, vulnerability, and transparency are all keys in finding Mirrors and uncovering connection. The more we risk, the greater the power from the Mirror Effect.

"There are no guarantees...
From the viewpoint of fear, none are strong enough.
From the viewpoint of love, none are necessary."
—Emmanuel Teney

Challenge #6 – Have You Gone Completely Mad?

One difficulty Mirrors encounter comes from the outside. Friends and family often are caught off-guard by the changes you are going through and the speed at which the relationship launches. If all of your life you've been super outgoing, outspoken, and have had tons of friends, and suddenly you've become much more reclusive (spending most of your time with your new Mirror), then your friends and family may perceive your new relationship negatively.

Caring, mixed with a lack of understanding, may cause them to confront you—sometimes vehemently. From their perspective, the change is so great, and so unexpected, that it *must* be bad. You may hear a variety of objections, including:

- How can someone change that much that fast?
- You can't possibly fall in love that quickly?!
- You can't possibly know yet!
- How can you already be engaged?
- Look what you've become since you've been with him!
- You hardly see us anymore.
- You're never this quiet.
- You're just a shadow of yourself.
- You hardly know her!
- You've only known each other for such a short time!
- It's just infatuation. It won't last.

This list, often accompanied with great emotional intensity, goes on and on. There is no knowledge from which they can draw to help them understand what you're going through, and likely nothing you can say will overcome their walls of misunderstanding.

What they fail to understand is that much of that outgoing, outspoken, gregarious person was compensation. A life that is unfulfilled at its center will find other avenues of fulfillment. A lonely heart will reach out to others to fill the day with conversation and the nights with communal connection. At the end of the day filled with laughter and friends and family, the house can still feel empty and so can the soul.

But when the heart and soul are filled by the deepest intimate connection, the need for external compensation evaporates. Meeting a Mirror allows the real person to come forward. Buried, maybe for an entire lifetime, is a person within who just wants peace, love, and connection. With the speed of a Mirror Relationship, you obtain your deepest desires nearly instantaneously. The relationship moves too quickly for those around you to keep pace. Even to the closest friends and family, the change you go through at the *soul level* may be unrecognizable. Where there should be elation for a heart's truest needs being met, instead harsh judgment is often rendered.

Pay no attention to the naysayers. You are likely to run into more than a few. Whether it is because they are envious of your love, are defending their less-than-Mirror-relationship, or simply misunderstand your shift, people will question your relationship. You, on the other hand, will rejoice because your heart is finally full, your life is full, and your love truly alive. Given time, even the naysayers will eventually come around.

A final note about the "madness" in Mirroring concerns the effects of the relationship on you. Discovering the Mirror love of your life creates a feeling of grounded euphoria. For a time your world will unhinge as the relationship overshadows everything else. Work, bills, eating, sleeping—it all just doesn't happen per the usual plan.

There is no need to worry; just enjoy the ride. Even in this love dumb stupor, the self-correcting Mirroring process will keep you on track and provide clarity.

Ketut, Elizabeth Gilbert's sage medicine man, noted that sometimes losing balance for love is part of the balance in life. Nothing could be truer.

Challenge #7 – The Same, but Different

The most amazing Mirroring paradox is this: Every Mirror is the same *and* uniquely different. Each Mirror you discover is, by definition, the same as you. The Mirrors you meet are therefore highly similar to one another. Simultaneously, each pairing you experience with a Mirror will have a unique dynamic. This results in each Mirror connection feeling somewhat the same and at the same time, different.

Be aware of sharing the comparisons of any old Mirrors you may have had with your current Mirror. Respect your partner's basic human desire to be individual and special.

Challenge #8 – The Most Advanced Relationship

The Mirror relationship is the most advanced type of relationship you can experience. There is speed, pressure, a heightened feeling of vulnerability, expectation, and significance; it is a fast climb up a steep mountain. The more you are prepared for it and the less you try to control it, the greater tranquility you will achieve—and the better your chances at success.

Remember to *breathe rather than react* through the process. You will communicate better, enjoy the journey more fully, live more authentically, and love more openly.

Exposing Relationship Myths

If you enter the Mirror realm carrying your same old preconceptions, you'll end up falling into the same old potholes. Mirror daters run the risk of not *believing* that they can achieve the summit because of the weight of all that has come before, because they worship an old gospel that is really nothing more than archaic myth.

Let's do some myth busting!

Myth #1 – Relationships Require Compromise

Bollocks! Traditional relationships are built upon a paradigm where deep matching is not declared from the beginning. This results in less-than-optimal relationships.

By selecting a *matched* paradigm, *the concept of mismatches is removed*.

Mirrors, by definition, are *matched*. There's no room for misunderstandings. In place of spending a lifetime of effort explaining your reasoning, you are astonished when you have to actually explain anything at all. Rather than avoiding a topic that typically leads to an argument, you begin to wonder what you will ever argue about. Instead of compromising to the middle, you're always in agreement.

The Mirror Effect produces something unprecedented: *The Effortless Relationship.*

> *"It's simplicity. I'm no longer trying to <u>do</u> anything. I've never worked at our relationship. And I've never had a relationship that I wasn't working on." —Judy*

Myth #2 – You Need to Self-improve to Be Worthy of a Great Relationship

If we are to believe the Oranges, we need to improve the person we are in order to have a successful relationship. So why wait? Get working on your past so you can be ready for your future. Their suggested relationship tips might include:

- Learn to deal with the triggers that are created by your past.
- Learn to communicate fully and effectively with your partner or spouse.
- Learn to argue fairly.
- Learn to be a better listener.

Do it now! Be the best you can be so that when the relationship opportunity appears, you'll be ready!

Doesn't all of that sound like a bad commercial? Does a personal growth workout come with a set of Ginsu knives? But wait—there's more they want you to do!

And there always is.

I'm all for striving to improve who we are. After all, personal growth is a part of life—part of why we're here. But, the notion that we must be better than we already are in order to have an ideal relationship is simply not true. It's impressed upon us that fears must be eliminated and weaknesses strengthened before we are worthy of love. But if that were the case, no one would be in relationships; we'd all be going straight from work to therapy or meditation or church (and don't forget your checkbook).

Here's an interesting question. Does someone who quibbles—a quibbler—need to learn how not to argue in order to be worthy of a superlative relationship?

The traditional consensus would conclude that the quibbler needs self-improvement to learn how to better communicate. It seems that most of us are not quibblers, so the tendency is to lean towards *fixing* the quibbler. Here's the number for Quibblers Anonymous, honey.

In the Mirror relationship, a quibbler would be matched to another quibbler. The quibbling Mirror couple isn't broken because they quibble; it is *who they are*! In fact, for them, it's not an argument but another form of communication. Quibbling is expected and anticipated; it fulfills a need! The quibbler couple happily banter the day long, processing situations and information in their unique way. Their pairing is actually quite harmonious, at least to them.

Our Mirrors find us *where we already are*. That doesn't mean to say that self-improvement is a bad thing; it's a good thing. But it's a myth that we must improve *first* to be worthy of great love.

Myth #3 – You Gotta Give That Up If You Want Someone

Many times when we enter a relationship, we change who we are in an attempt to make ourselves a better fit. We change our behavior, trying to make a new "best us" that more readily fits the relationship dynamic.

The artist stops painting because his partner complains it takes too much time away from their relationship. Now the artist is left with a void in his inner core.

A woman who needs deep love and physical contact shares a relationship with a man who is less intimate, and so she becomes less intimate. She is left feeling lonely and physically abandoned.

A partner gives up her group of friends because he is an introvert. She is left feeling disconnected from the essential nourishment of friends.

A little bit of us—some part of the soul—dies when we lose an inner part of ourselves. Sadly those surrendered parts are often our most amazing natural gifts—lost to bad pairings. A tender heart, the craftsman, the artist, whatever it is that is special, is lost because our partner's traits, needs, or desires are not in alignment with our gifts. This creates sadness, and eventually leads to resentment and regret, for we have sacrificed an innate part of who we are.

Whatever it is for each of us, our Mirror allows our innate characteristics to naturally emerge. We begin to live the person, the true fiber, of who we truly are—unsuppressed, unchanged, unmodified—when we are with a Mirror. Quibbler, emotional, tender, harsh, easily-moved, meek, strong—whatever defines us is accepted and amplified.

Myth #4 – Our Partners Don't Complete Us

When I started meeting Judy's friends, they all gave me "that look". The look that says, "You have no idea what you're in for. Just you wait." They told me about this strong woman with whom I shared a beautiful relationship. They said my brilliant CEO could be difficult, prone to fits of anger, strong, willful, and often too direct.

Funny, I don't know that person. *Who is she?* The Judy I know is open, tender, loving, and has a huge heart.

It was immediately obvious that the Mirror Effect was at work.

With me, Judy is more of her true self than she has ever been in her life. Her long-repressed sensitive side flows like an ancient river that has resurfaced—her heart is open fully and she is more alive than any time in her life. Even when facing the world, her friends and people around her feel the dramatic shift. Her life was already potent and dynamic. Now it is even more so, amplified beyond what she even imagined to be possible.

Now Judy's friends look at me and say, "Who is this person and what have you done with Judy Day?"

In a time where we're told that the only way to receive a full relationship is to be complete in ourselves, with a Mirror relationship we discover that our partners *do* complete us—and in ways that are deep and significant.

THE ULTIMATE PAIRING

Magical Matches are the ultimate pairings. The Mirror Effect creates a pairing synergy that pulls our best traits forward and a relationship dynamic that replaces friction with ease, discord with peace, uncertainty with assuredness, and ambivalence with deeply seated soulful love.

Beginning with the first meeting, the Mirror Effect creates the Everest of relationships. From the summit, a Mirror pairing is a thing of grace and beauty. The view is pure and awe-inspiring—the panorama of your life together is unobstructed. To stand on the roof of the world with your Magical Match is an unparalleled experience, a climb to the most amazing relationship of your life.

Key Concepts
- The Mirror Effect describes, defines, and explains the extraordinary relationship shared by Mirrors.
- Mirrors are two people who are so extremely alike in sharing a single heart, mind, and soul that it feels as though they are looking into a mirror reflection of each other.
- A Mirror relationship is a different type of pairing that leads to soul-deep love and a relationship of ease.

- Mirror relationships have new rules and challenges that are in most ways much simpler than the traditional relationship rules and challenges. Many times these rules and challenges are completely opposite of our understanding of relationships.

Mirror Effect Laws
- If it's work, it's wrong.
- People will believe that you've gone mad.
- Every Mirror is the same, but also different.
- You don't choose the relationship; the relationship chooses you.
- Sometimes love is not enough.
- You have many Mirrors.
- A Mirror relationship is the most advanced relationship you can experience.

PART 2

6 STEPS TO FINDING YOUR MAGICAL MATCH

7

WORLD-WIDE-DATING

"Is there anywhere else in our lives where we voluntarily put ourselves through so much discomfort and pain than in dating? I mean really....daters are miserable! If dating were a disease, most of us would have filed a DNR order! If I suffer a coronary during one more inane date-opening summary of today's weather, just leave me there dead. Maybe dating in the afterlife will be easier!"

Online dating has revolutionized the way we seek relationships in much the same way the Internet has revolutionized the way we find information in general. Before the Internet, information was gathered slowly, printed in books and then placed into libraries or bookstores. Performing research meant going to the places where the books were in order to find the desired information. The same was true for finding a partner. Finding a mate meant going somewhere: college, church, the grocery store, work, bars, the dog park, or to group activities. But with these in-person venues, your dating pool was always limited—and so was your chance of finding an ideal pairing.

The Web changes everything. Searching for information is just a few key clicks away. Moreover, finding even the most esoteric information is easy and practically immediate. With the Web and the correct search tool (a web browser), the entire catalog of information pools into a single accessible location—the screen right in front of you.

Why should our approach to dating be any different? If we can pool, filter, and select all of the available people into a single, searchable location, why would we avoid doing it? What is the potential of finding an ideal pairing among *millions* instead of the 500 people that attend your church or the 50 who show up at your local dog park?

For our parents, aunts and uncles, let alone generations before them, *finding* a Mirror relationship was nothing short of a miracle—an incredible stroke of luck. *No more!* Online dating now gives us access to millions of people, and therefore millions of possibilities. Used strategically and appropriately, in conjunction with the Mirror Effect, online dating may very well redefine everything we know about meeting, matching, and, ultimately, relationships. We just need to have *the right mindset and the right target.* We need to have a dating *formula.* And that's exactly what these 6 steps will help you do.

8

STEP 1 – THE MIRROR PROFILE

A profile is not a marketing tool, it's a filter!

"Two strangers square off for a first date; the restaurant table instantly transforms into a ballpark. Like a pitcher, the daters lob pitches to the other side of the table. Nothing too hard or fast. The easiest thing possible so that he might have a chance to hit it out of the ballpark. 'I like pizza.' Yeah! Let's see if he connects with that one. OMG! He clobbered it! AND he's gorgeous! I think there's real potential for this relationship."

Traditional profiles turn first dates into blind expeditions for matching.

BUILT TO FAIL

So you've selected an online dating site, taken the time to post your best pictures, and plunked down some hard-earned cash. You've even made an investment in writing your profile—spent all day at it, as a matter of fact. And it turned out something like this:

I enjoy music, movies, a glass of wine, walks on the beach, dining out, dancing, and traveling. I am fit, love my job (mostly) and am financially secure. I seek an attractive man/ woman to share life and love. Someone who is humorous, kind, and knows how to treat me well. If any of this describes you, drop me an email. Yadda, yadda, yadda...

How's that workin' for ya? Not too well, I betcha. Mine was similar when I started online dating.

Pictures, declaring logistics, purchasing the subscription—those are all pretty easy. Almost universally, the profile is the most difficult part of creating your online presence. Generally, people just don't know how to write about themselves in a way that will be understood. Instead of clarity, profiles become poorly written descriptions that bear nearly identical content.

Let's examine what happens from a practical viewpoint when a database is filled with homogeneous data.

Consider how a Google search would work if every web site contained exactly the same words. Imagine how many different, and completely irrelevant, websites would result from your search if you entered *music* or *travel* or *kind*? How long would it take for you to become completely disenfranchised with the idea of surfing the Web for answers if your searches never returned useful results?

The same problem applies to online dating when the profiles are virtually indistinguishable from each other. There are no search words to find your perfect guy when *every* profile says, "I am a man." There is no hope of finding a superlative pairing when you have to date every male on the dating site to determine which guy is The One. Manually sorting millions of profiles (or people) is an impossible task.

What's worse is that when the first step is poorly executed, the entire process suffers a cascading failure:

- We search through the online database looking for something unique.
- Because the database is populated with millions of nearly identical profiles, the search returns millions of useless results.
- To compensate, we read *every* profile searching for someone to love in megabytes of uninteresting, uninspired, nondescript drivel.

- Predictably, we tire of reading profiles.
- So we stop reading.
- It doesn't take long before no one actually *reads* anyone else's profile.
- Instead, we turn restaurant tables into baseball stadiums, blindly looking for *anything* that matches.
- Invariably, the long-hit ball does not translate into long-term love, and soon it's back to sorting through the drivel.

And you wonder why date after date you're not succeeding at finding lasting love, or even getting closer to it?

Without profiles that are clear and unique, online dating (mostly) fails to deliver its promise of finding great pairings.

WE NEED TO BUILD A FILTER

The problem is that we have yet to learn how to properly employ the online dating tool. Because it's the first step in the process, and the entire foundation for the search engine, the profile is the single most critical item for the online dater. In order to properly exploit the power of online dating, we must master the online profile by learning:

- *how* to write
- *what* to write
- and the *purpose* for which it is being written
- so that searches return usable results.

As everything in the Mirror Effect works opposite to the traditional, we'll start at the bottom of the list and work in reverse. Let's take the first big step in using the online dating tool properly by examining the *purpose* of an online profile.

The Fewer, the Better

Most people view their online profile's purpose as marketing. They drone on about their closest companion (the dog) and their full, happy lives (except that they're single) and expect their view counter to climb like votes tabulated for an American Idol contestant. And when their profile counters don't increase quickly enough, they broaden their profile in an attempt to increase marketability and attract even more people. The results are a self-defeating process with little or no valuable connections and endless hours of wasted time.

Although seemingly counterintuitive, *fewer hits are better.* Any successful salesperson will say that a single qualified lead is more valuable than 100 cold calls. Look at it from their perspective—time is money. Salespeople abhor wasting time on dead-end leads. They want leads that are prepared to transact. *They want results!* Results are the only things that count at the end of the day—or in the evening when you head out for a date. Just like a sales person ought to filter potential clients whose needs best reflect what his product offers, serious daters want to filter for people who Mirror and reflect them.

The purpose for a profile is to filter the dating pool down to your Mirrors. When you build the right words into your profile, others will:

- be able to search properly
- find and read your profile
- contact you if there is potential
- move on if there isn't a possible match

With the right profile, most people will self-sort; the entire dating-pool will automatically reduce in size. And believe it or not, this is *exactly* what you want.

It's All in the Reflection

You can forget everything that you think you know about profiles. Any profile that contains

- "My friends and family say..."
- "About me? Let's see, I love to..."
- "What I'm looking for in a partner is..."

is about as useful as a bowling ball with no holes.

To find a Mirror relationship, you must write a profile that is a reflection of you. Not the old ideas of what you thought you wanted in a partner, but a profile about who you really are inside. A Mirror Profile describes your beliefs, feelings, ideals, and life perspectives—the aspects that define your core self.

When your profile is read, you will then attract others who share your same core facets. Your prose will resonate deeply, touching a place much deeper than any other words they've ever read. They will respond with an, "OMG—that's me! How can anyone know me like that?" When they see themselves in the reflection created by your profile, they will be moved within and compelled to send an emphatic response.

Even though we're in the realm of engineering matches, a profile is still partially art, inherently ethereal. The following suggestions can help you bridge the gap between science and art.

Facets of the Soul

When writing your profile, it is important to focus on inner qualities rather than external habits, hobbies or interests. The first and most important tier of Mirroring is to reflect at the soul level. The following is a list of some of the most important characteristics for Mirroring:

- **Personal Energy Level**: How much do you like to keep on the move with work, projects, activities, and hobbies? How much do you like to rest and take it easy? Are you more of a type A or B personality? Be honest about where and how you spend your time and energy.

- **Ambition**: Are you driven to achieve social status, fame, power or wealth? How ambitious are you and what type of life do you aspire to have?

- **Money & Materialism**: How do you view, make, save, and spend money? Are you materialistic, wanting the best of things, or do you strive for a simple non-materialistic life? Or are you some place in between? Honestly describe your relationship to money and things.

- **Emotional Intimacy**: What does emotional intimacy in a relationship mean to you? How would you describe the type of emotional intimacy you want in your relationship?

- **Risk and Caution**: How much risk do you like in your life? How much caution? In what aspects of your life do you easily take risks? Where do you prefer a more cautious approach?

- **Romantic Encounters**: In the realm of dating and relationships, do you prefer to take it slow with a look-before-you-leap attitude? Or are you more spontaneous and impulsive? Describe what feels best and comfortable to you.

- **Outlook—Pessimistic or Optimistic**: Are you a Pollyanna optimist, an Eeyore pessimist, or somewhere in between? How would you describe yourself in relationship to your worldview?

- **Sexual / Libido**: Describe how often you like sexual encounters with your partner and what you are looking for in a sexual relationship.

- **Passion**: Are you a passionate, intense person, an even-keeled person, or are your feelings more on the mild side?

- **Nurturing**: How often and in what way do you like to nurture your partner?

- **Togetherness**: When in a relationship, how much of your free time do you want to spend with your partner? Most of it, half, less than half? Do you prefer to spend time with just the two of you or do you need a lot of social time as well?

- **Intellectual Stimulation**: Aside from your established areas of expertise, do you hunger for learning? Are you intrigued by new ideas and information? What do you find intellectually stimulating? How much time, if any, do you spend on new ideas and information?

- **Artistic Appreciation**: Do you make art and culture an ongoing part of your life? Is music, art or nature's beauty among life's greatest pleasures for you? If so, describe the ways you engage in this arena of life, and why.

- **Idealism, Spirituality and Humanity**: Are you more idealistic or realistic about life? Do you think life is fair? Do you believe people generally get what they deserve or are circumstances more fair to some than others? What are your attitudes on political and social issues? What kind of responsibility, if any, do you feel you have to help others or to make things better in the world?

- **Head vs. Heart**: When in a relationship, are you more in your head than your heart? Or are you more in your heart than your head? When wanting to connect with your partner, are you more inclined to be centered in your feelings or your head?

- **Values**: A great way to find out what you value is to look at where you spend the majority of your time and energy. Using this filter, what are the things you value most highly in life?

- **Religion / Spirituality**: Do you belong to a religion or spiritual community? Do you have an important spiritual or religious practice? If so, describe what it is, its role in your life, and how involved you are with it.

- **Type of relationship sought**: Are you looking for a traditional relationship with traditional roles, a relationship of equals, or any of the 31 flavors in between? How would you describe the type of relationship you are looking for?

Writing Your Profile

Write about your relationship to each of the 15 core Facets of the Soul. Start with a few sentences that describe the way you feel about and express each of these facets. Describe what matters most to you about each one. When considering a core facet, it can be helpful to think about what it is about that facet that brings you joy, energy and excitement. Try beginning your sentences with starter phrases like these:

I am.....	I like...	I love....	I enjoy...
I believe...	I appreciate...	I wish....	I often...
I feel...	I never...	I tend to...	I wish I could...
I need...	I seldom...	I don't....	I think...
I wonder...	I must...	I want...	I might be found...

Be as honest and open as you can. The goal is to express the deepest parts of you.

Once you've written your "I" statements, transform them into "you" questions: "Are you...?" or "Do you....? This way your finished profile will ask your potential Mirrors if they see themselves in your words.

Once you've completed the first draft of your profile, reread what you've written and ask yourself these questions to see if you have really hit the mark:

- Does my profile accurately describe me?
- Does it describe my soul facets—who I am at my core?
- Does it include what's most important to me?
- Have I spell-checked my profile?

Include a short introduction. Before you post your profile, write a brief opening to let your readers (potential Mirrors) know what you are looking for. Here is an example:

"The following profile describes me, as well as what I am looking for in a partner. Please let me know if you see yourself in my words—what parts of my profile move you, resonate with you, or don't fit. If you deeply recognize yourself in what I've written here, please contact me as I think we may share a very profound connection."

Remember, a good Mirror profile is a work in progress. Take notes from each date or relationship. Write about the parts that deeply touched you. Note where you saw yourself, specifically where the best parts of you were pulled forward. Use your experiences to continue to polish the reflection of your Mirror, creating an even more refined filter.

A FINAL NOTE – KEYS TO THE HEART

Every person has a set of imperative needs, a list of things they require in order to make them feel alive and deeply connected in a relationship. These are essential air to the soul and without them we cannot breathe in the fullness of life and love. We call these, *The Keys to Your Heart.*

To discover the Keys to your Heart, ask yourself:

- What is it that I absolutely can't live without?
- In a relationship, what makes me feel the most alive, loved, seen, and cherished?
- What's the most important way I communicate my deepest feelings to someone I love?
- What matters the most to me?

Make it a point to ask about your date's Keys, preferably on the first date. Even if your date doesn't know what you're referring to or has never thought about it before, it's an opening for a meaningful conversation. To demonstrate what you mean, share your own Keys. Here are some examples:

- Touch. I absolutely require touch.
- I require an adventurous companion.
- I give what I want to receive.
- I need to be empathized with and understood.
- I need someone whose ideas spark my own.

Keys are another type of filter. If your Keys are in some way reflected or deeply understood, you're certainly in the Mirror domain with your date. If not, then it's not likely good pairing potential as a Magical Match.

NOW THAT I HAVE MY PROFILE, WHERE SHOULD I POST IT?

Open Sites

Websites like match.com and plentyoffish.com are a great venue for a wide Mirror search. Members of open sites select largely based upon your profile's content. When you use a Mirror Profile on one of these sites, you will attract people with the highest level of matching—those that can lead to mind-blowing first date connections. Here are some tips to maximize your results:

- Give your profile up to three months to begin to work, and then up to 6 months to filter to the strongest Mirrors.
- Resist the urge to create more hits by morphing your filter into marketing.
- Expect about three good hits a month once the profile takes hold. Mirror connections compel an investment in time—you'd be surprised that three responses a month is probably more than you can handle because connections will be much deeper.
- Be patient.

Guided Matching Sites

Guided matching sites, like eHarmony and Chemistry, concentrate on *personality matching*—a guided online dating experience, presenting only those who are matched on a deeper level. Matching software is a hidden gem. With sites like these, you are often required to answer a fairly long list of questions in order for their matching algorithm to function. In addition, there are always some areas of the site in which subscribers provide a short essay(s) about themselves.

The essay areas are the targets for your Mirror Profile. Regardless of how the site is constructed, place your Mirror Profile in the essay areas. If necessary, segment your profile into smaller chunks and place it in the separate essay boxes (if the areas are limited to a particular number of words). The idea is to get your Mirror Profile on your profile page so that others can see it. This might look a little strange to other members because you're using the site in an unconventional manner, but that's okay. Your personal Mirror

Profile filter is far better than any form answer! Those who Mirror you will see the beauty behind your words.

Combining your Mirror Profile with an online site that uses matching software is an excellent step towards finding your Magical Match.

There's No Time Like the Present

Building a Mirror Profile isn't difficult. Remember, it's all about you and who you are inside. With a couple of pointers and a little imagination, your Mirror Profile will appear on the page before you know it.

"The process of the profile writing itself has created unexpected excitement and increased commitment to getting what I want. For a long time, I was reluctant and resistant to writing my profile at all. I couldn't imagine being successful, so I found myself afraid to get into the game at all. I was afraid that I might not be resilient enough to recover quickly from the drama and rejections that dating involves. I got support from close friends and finally made myself sit down and at least come up with a first draft. When I saw my match described in black and white, I experienced myself feeling excited to know him. It made me look...not half bad! If these were the best of my qualities, translated into a man, I became very enthusiastic to seek and meet him! If this is actually what I get to have, I WANT him ASAP!"

Key Concepts

- The Mirror Profile is the first step in Mirroring and is the foundation of the Mirroring Process.
- Your profile should be a deep, clear reflection of *who you are*. Whether it is just a list of questions or a complex missive, a Mirror Profile is the first-stage filter for creating a smaller, better-matched dating pool from the millions.
- A Mirror Profile alleviates the need to market yourself. There is no need to create or be imaginative; you only need to describe who you are inside. There is no need to sell yourself—your words create a mirror. Mirroring is much deeper than any marketing.
- The fewer, the better. When the filter is working properly, you will have fewer responses and dates. That's a good thing.
- When you start your online dating path from a different place, you end up with completely different results.

Mirror Effect Laws

- Know yourself. The search for a Magical Match begins *inside*, not outside.

Steps Towards Your Magical Match

- Use the online dating tool properly by starting with a Mirror Profile.
- As you learn more about yourself, modify the profile appropriately. The purpose of modification should only be to strengthen the clarity of the reflection that others see.

- Use your profile on all online dating sites.
- Be mindful of your logistical criteria, such as distance, race, religion, children, economics, education, etc. Each criterion should be aligned with your preferences. These are also a part of the mirror. Don't break your mirror by configuring your search parameters outside of your natural inclinations.
- Ask about the *Keys To Your Heart*. You need to be sure that your Mirror has the ability to satisfy your Keys.

9

STEP 3 - FILTER
Mirroring is about filtering, not casting a wide net

"The Law of Averages is not a formula component of the Laws of Mirroring. Kissing a hundred frogs is more likely to give you bad breath and a hankerin' for dipping sauce than to put you any closer to finding your Magical Match."

To understand why so many online daters fail, let's take a look into Kim's dating history. Kim is a teacher in a culinary institute and the single mother of an eight-year-old son. Kim has been an online dater for several years. She's attractive, fun, happy, has a positive attitude and great energy, *but* she still hasn't found a relationship that works for her. Kim has tried everything—bars, friends of friends, Facebook, the grocery store, online dating. Her next scheme? *Date Las Vegas style!* Kim's plan is to date as many men as possible in the shortest amount of time.

- Kim's dating strategy: Play the odds
- Kim's ante: Two years of her life
- Kim's bet: 55 first dates

Kim steps into the dating casino and tries the numbers game. He *is* out there; she just has to find him. By playing the odds, *eventually* she will strike gold, right?

Wrong!

Kim spent two years of her life dating every man who came to the table. *Two years!* That translates to 104 weeks, which, on average, equates to a *first date every other week!* That's exhausting to just think about. You have to admire her determination and, simultaneously, consider entering a plea of insanity on her behalf. Although Kim might find her Magical Match by constantly tossing the dice, she has about the same odds of meeting Elvis while dancing the Macarena in the zoo's alligator pen.

Kim's dating strategy returned nothing but despair, disillusionment, heartbreak, and a deeply seated feeling that she should just give up. There wasn't even a consolation prize. She left Vegas broke, bitter, and unwed.

The Real Solution is Filtering

The answer to winning the numbers game isn't to date as many people as possible, but rather to date as *few* as possible. In order to reach the goal of finding a Magical Match, Kim, and anyone else seeking their Magical Match, needs to create an environment wherein they date only those who are the best candidates by:

- Reducing the size of the dating pool
- Providing a measure to qualify candidates
- Dating only those who qualify

Reducing the Size of the Dating Pool

From Step 1: Mirror Profile, you already know that the Mirror Profile is a self-selecting system that automatically draws forward your Mirrors, creating a select pool from which to date. This is the first-stage filter.

Measuring Candidates

Some people who are not Mirrors will probably still respond to your online profile. Maybe they identify with just one or two statements in your profile and think that's enough. Heck, they may not even read your profile and respond based only on physical attraction. Because of this, you need a way to *measure* each candidate's responses to ensure he or she is a Mirror. *Learning how to measure these responses is the key to filtering.*

The Mirror Effect has an element of *astonishment*. When we see ourselves reflected in the words of a profile there is a feeling of recognition and awe. *How could that profile describe me so well? Who is this person? How can someone know so many of my deepest thoughts and feelings?*

The element of astonishment compels an emphatic response that is readily recognizable. Rather than a Wink or light opening, a committal response is much more likely:

- Wow! What you wrote was unbelievable! Reading your profile was like a breath of fresh air. You described me so well."
- What an incredibly well written and thought-provoking profile you've created.... I'm very impressed with your thinking. Best one I've read or that I'll probably ever read by far. You have certainly touched my heart. I'm looking for a unique individual, one who captures my "essence" and you seem to do just that.
- Your profile resonates with me. There are many places in your profile where we match. I'd love to explore the possibilities.
- When I read your profile it spoke to me. You have captured my attention! Are you real?

Don't these responses seem different than the run-of-the-mill ones that you instantly delete from your inbox? You know, the ones that say, "Hi. You have a nice smile. I want to meet you" or "Hello, I liked your profile. I love dogs, too." See how much easier is it to separate the connected responses from the rest? The Mirror Profile not only simultaneously attracts and filters, but it also provides a framework for responses to be measured and evaluated. *Wait! That's actually scientific!* Science and online dating? Einstein meets Liz Taylor!

Even when you are the one initiating contact, you can still use your profile as a filter and a means to measure candidates. As you are searching through profiles, look for ones that have some element that Mirrors you. Then, reach out to them with a message that asks them to read your profile. For example:

- "Hi there! Your profile completely spoke to me. We really seem to have similar thoughts about x, y, z. I invite you to read my profile. I'd love to hear from you if it resonates with you."

The stage is set. If there is no response, then it's not a Mirror. If there is correspondence, keep digging until you've decided there is a possible Mirror. If the eventual response is emphatic, you'll know there is something meaningful to investigate.

If you're not sure, you can use the following questions as a guide. If all the answers are yes, there's probably enough of a connection to warrant a first date:

- Did he/she read your Mirror Profile?
- Was the reaction emphatic?
- Is there a strong Mirroring with a majority of the profile?
- Are the logistics aligned?

Measuring Candidates is the second-stage filter. In evaluating the responses, you'll validate the first-stage filter and once again decrease the size of the dating pool.

Date Only the Qualified

Once you've crafted your Mirror Profile, stick to it! Filter every person you wish to date through the essence of your profile. Whether you meet someone at the mailbox, in the dentist's office, in the grocery store, or online—each of them first receives a copy of your Mirror Profile before dating commences. After all the effort, why would you date an unqualified candidate? Before I met Judy for our second first date, I asked her to reread my profile. I knew that commitment to the Filter Step provides a key element in a self-correcting process that would bring me better pairings from which to select. Dating only the qualified is the third-stage filter.

A Final Note on Filtering

Not all opening communications will be intense or deep. Some might be a quick note, or in the case of Match.com the opening salvo can be nothing more than a Wink. If that's the case, you can filter further by responding with, "Thanks for the Wink! Is there something about my profile that resonates with you?" Continue digging until you're able to qualify the candidate as a Mirror.

When we apply the Mirror Effect as a *filter*, the results are substantial. Using our reflection to sort through the entire dating population identifies Mirrors, eliminates those who are not, and creates a pool of highly Mirrored people from which to select.

Playing the odds with a deck stacked with winners is the only way to beat the odds in Vegas!

Key Concepts

- *Reducing* the size of the pool to those who are highly mirrored *increases* the odds of finding a Magical Match.
- Filtering, combined with a Mirror Profile, creates an environment for emphatic responses.
- Filtering actually begins when you write your profile, and it continues to influence the rest of your journey in the Mirroring Process.

Mirror Effect Law

- The Law of Averages does not apply to the Mirror Effect. Don't play the odds.

Steps Towards Your Magical Match

- Filter, filter, filter! *Every* potential date *must* be filtered through your Mirror Profile.
- Date only when there is clear reflection with your Mirror. Look for the emphatic response.
- Date only those that have successfully passed through the filter.

10

STEP 3 - CONNECTION

The purpose of Mirror Dating is not to build a connection, but to discover if one already exists

As the sun sets on another warm evening, she appears at the door. The café is quiet, romantically lit by dappled sunlight dancing on the tabletops like shimmering water. An introduction, a smile, a timid hug initiate another first date. Tucked into a secluded corner, we settle in at the table. Fiddling with the menu holds nervous energy; the dialogue meanders as aimlessly as the plates on the arms of a wayward waiter, both looking for the right place to land. But as twilight beckons, a moment sparks as she begins a tale that isn't hers alone.

Suddenly, something extraordinary happens. The conversation deepens. Each word, every thought, rings through as the hidden pages of your life are revealed by another. Gravity pulls inward as the connection begins to take hold. Time slows as the first touch of hands reveals what the heart is beginning to feel. The river, ever moving in-between, begins to still; a reflection begins to appear. And as she speaks her deepest feelings—your deepest feelings—the sensation of intense astonishment would be overwhelming but for the bond of a quickening connection.

The hands, once just touching, embrace each other. And as you stare, lost in connection, it is not the eyes that you see, but the soul, heart, and mind. You begin to understand her, just as you understand yourself. Time hangs, suspending the river of connection into perfect calm. Staring into each other's eyes, holding hands across the table, there is perfect symmetry, each a mirror of the other—just as the mirrored reflection in the now timeless, motionless water. And as she slips deeper into her heart to tell its love and dreams, a kiss across the table seals the connection into bond.

You've just met a Mirror...

Dating is a journey of a thousand miles that begins with a first date. Food, drinks, candles, and conversation hopefully create a romantic balance to something that is, if we're honest, part exploration, part interrogation. Autobiographies are the opening paragraphs in the language of discovery between two strangers seeking to find companionship for life's long journey. Words, passing just as the minutes, attempt to describe the truth of a life. And in those precious first moments is the opportunity to discover the most valued first-date element—*connection.*

Connection is what happens when we meet a Mirror. Connection is everything. Connection is the fuel that propels a couple forward. Connection imparts confidence in what is normally a guarded sea of doubt. Connection brings a relationship to life, animating its existence. Connection is a bond, the window through which *potential* shines. Connection opens a greater depth of sharing and allows us to see the promise of a relationship, which creates anticipation. Ultimately, a deep connection gives us hope and courage to begin the journey together.

Openness – The Path to Connection

If one had to describe in a single word the mindset for the traditional first date it would likely be *caution.* Repeated failures and heartbreak result in daters hiding behind protective walls, blocking avenues to connection. Experience makes daters wary. To compensate, months of dating are required to establish a feeling of safety before the true, authentic person can surface. But this is no guarantee. Even after investing in the long, slow, steady climb together, we too seldom reach the summit. Failure, it seems, has favored odds when we approach relationships with caution.

Caution has another face. Somewhere in our past, we've learned that relationships are *built*. The cautious tendency is to supply just enough about ourselves to attract, but not so much that it will frighten—frighten ourselves and our partner. Popular dating wisdom would advise you to measure yourself out slowly, test carefully, and hold back anything that might not keep them interested.

These are tactics that attempt to *create* connection by controlling both the pace and the content of a budding relationship. It's as if we believe that openly sharing everything will somehow cause the connection *not* to form, or that it takes time for a connection to form.

Mirroring is not about *building* connection. The first date is a meeting to discover if two people unknowingly *already* share a connection. Discovering that connection requires a different mindset: *transparency*.

It is a simple equation. Allowing someone to see and touch your soul creates an environment of genuine trust, honesty, and safety. When you become transparent, it allows your date to also become transparent. Within total openness, exploration and discovery are uncomplicated. It's much easier to discover connection, to see reflection, when there is nothing blocking the view.

Helen (my first mirror) and I shared a deep, soulful connection *before* we met. Our Mirror connection had probably existed for our entire lives. But a typical first date wouldn't have been enough to discover it. What if Helen had decided to go no deeper than the weather? Would a date filled with current events, past marriages, current jobs, and the story of the neighborhood dogs have provided the magic combination? Unlikely. But when she began to speak of her life, the challenges she had faced growing up, the lack of love, her life perspective, her meek demeanor—everything from her soul—the reflection appeared. If she had not been brave enough to share her very core, our Mirror connection would have gone undiscovered. Complete transparency amplified the Mirror Effect, creating a deep reflection in which I could see myself.

The more we opened up, the more connection we discovered. In turn, the power of connection made it possible to open even further. A self-reinforcing cycle of connection and openness fueled an exploration of the *depth and breadth* of our connection. Common beliefs, mentality, spirituality, life perspectives—anything and everything was on the table. We even discussed sexual likes and dislikes! Try approaching that particular subject on a typical first date and see how far you get!

If we go back and take another look at the email thread between Judy and me, we can see another great example of openness and transparency. Recall that this exchange occurred *before* we met for our "second" first date:

From: Judy Day
Sent: Thursday, July 15, 2010 2:54 PM
To: 'Troy Pummill'
Subject: FW: A Summer Personal Growth Workout!

Just curious, does this type of event have interest to you?

From: Troy Pummill
Sent: Thursday, July 15, 2010 3:59 PM
To: 'Judy Day'
Subject: RE: A Summer Personal Growth Workout!!

Judy,
...I believe it's important to acknowledge truths, even as they may be couched within. It seems as if we're both interested in more than just friends getting together; there seems to be facets of exploring...
...More to your question, I don't spend time working on myself in the ways that I know you do. My spirituality, my depth, is more

organic. With the right match, the right heart and soul—I'm quite deep and emotionally available, sensitive, compassionate, and loving, especially for a male. For me, love and touch are essential. So is romance. I've been told that I have a high EQ. My problem has (mostly) been finding a partner who is ready to meet me in the deep canyon that is my heart and soul. In those deep places, I lay there waiting—open, yearning—for a woman whose heart is as deep as mine. Truly amazing, deep, wonderful, joyous, connected intimacy follows, in every way....

Long, and genuine, answer to your question. lol

Does that help?

For what does your heart yearn, Judy?

My reply to her question is bold, open, and transparent. Since intimate connections are part of my Mirror, her email provided an opportunity to see how she would respond to this Mirror element.

I asked Judy about her heart's desire to discover if she had an emotional depth to match mine. It presented an avenue for her to be open in a way that would be meaningful for any Mirroring we share.

From: Judy Day
Sent: Friday, July 16, 2010 10:41 AM
To: 'Troy Pummill'
Subject: RE: A Summer Personal Growth Workout!

What a great email and I am laughing out loud. I suppose I am pretty transparent.

Yes, I am oriented to meeting you with an exploring mind not only just catching up.

Just so you know I did "break up" with John about 10 days ago. And we still have a friendship and work relationship. It will go through a lot of changes in the next few months I am sure. And I know I need time to process it all and transition.

I love the question—what does your heart yearn for? I have been pondering that recently. If you would like I'll let you know what I have so far on Saturday.

The openness in my email created a venue for her authentic reply. There is honesty in admitting the purpose of our meeting. Coupled with her releasing her boyfriend, the door is open and the stage set for discovering connection.

Note here, too, the Mirror Effect of accelerated time. In her head Judy thought she would need time to "process it all." In fact, she fell in love with me on our second first date. Hours, not weeks or months.

From: Troy Pummill
Sent: Friday, July 16, 2010 2:27 PM
To: 'Judy Day'
Subject: RE: A Summer Personal Growth Workout!

You've got me laughing. Transparency is a gift, even though many side to the contrary. There are gifts all around us, if we but have eyes to see them.

Thanks for sharing about John; certainly does provide some clarity and understanding. Know that I am sensitive to your ending, and also strongly believe that things come in the time they are meant to be. If it is our time, then the path will be illuminated by our uniqueness regardless of where we are at this very moment.

Since we are officially exploring (lol...how funny is that?), I think it's a probably a good idea to start at the beginning.

This is my profile. It has been an excellent tool in finding those who match me well. Would you be willing to have a read?

I'd love to know your reaction to it. Is it a Mirror for you? Do you see yourself in it? Mildly resonates? Goosebumps? Nausea?

Genuinely looking forward to tomorrow and hearing your heart's yearnings. I will be listening...

In this response, transparency and openness continue in the form of authenticity. I truly believe that transparency is a gift. Also, my response contains my Mirror elements of perspective and faith: I believe that circumstances happen for a purpose and with perfect timing.

And even though Judy and I had already met, I *always* employed the Mirroring Processes of profiling and filtering. If her response hadn't indicated she had Mirrored qualities, I had planned to cancel the date. I never dated where there wasn't a strong Mirror reflection.

From: Judy Day
Sent: Friday, July 16, 2010 5:17 PM
To: 'Troy Pummill'
Subject: Your Profile

I love the openness and vulnerability of your profile. I also love that you are really clear on what you want. The fact that you are looking for a deep committed relationship and willing to work on it is extremely attractive. And it is amazing that with just these two qualities you are not bombarded (or maybe you are) with women. After all this is what most women say they want. And even as I write that I know better.

I believe the type of relationship you are talking about is both possible and rare. I also believe that before being able to be in such a connection, you need to know yourself very well and be able to be present and available. And you have to actually want it enough to make it a priority and to surrender to it.

So yes, your profile resonates with me and scares me. No hint of nausea, but a lot of curiosity. To be honest I was in bed last night asking myself, "If I were on my deathbed and declared that my life ,had not been a total success, where would I have fallen short?" Here is what I came up with:

I never had a long lasting, loving, fun, committed relationship with a man who I surrendered into love with. A relationship where we created our best life accordingly to what was true and real and alive within us.

I never fully became and expressed my full capacity for compassion, peace, and love.

These were the two biggest so I will leave it here.

The openness of this entire email correspondence creates an environment for Judy's unreserved, boldly authentic reply. She is completely open and vulnerable about her past relationships, her heart, and, essentially, what she wants in a relationship.

From my side, there is resonance and a strong Mirror. Judy frames her answer in a way that says she understands what's important in life. That is a direct Mirror of me. Compassion, peace and love are Mirrored qualities. In her acknowledging her need for self-knowledge, presence, and availability, Judy tells me that she expects and understands the same things I do about relationships. She is open and vulnerable, communicative, bold and expressive—another Mirror for me.

Her response is dead on target. Cupid has upgraded from bow and arrow to laser-guided love missile!

And all this transparency began from the very first step of the Mirroring Process. The Mirror Profile, a declaration in openness, initiates the Mirror Effect and illuminates connection and potential. Continued openness throughout the communication process—whether via email, phone, text, IM, or in person—provides the environment for a Mirror connection to be revealed.

THE POWER OF CONNECTION

The Mirror Connection is an indescribable, undeniable, nearly cosmic force that defies explanation:

"Dawn and I started off with an email that said, 'That was amazing!' The Mirror Effect struck Dawn deeply, my profile resonating soulful chords within her. It was as if someone had read from the deepest places within her heart. She was compelled to reach out—and so our connection began. Emails

filled with beautiful thoughts and quotes that held personal deep meaning that reflected so strongly. A language of emotional touching continued into unending phone conversations—the connection's depth revealed more with each day. Dawn was all I could think about, like having a piece of my soul missing. Work, eating, at the movies, commuting—the connection was always there. It didn't take long for the emotional, romantic connection to naturally progress to sexual within the gravity that bonded us together. What had started out as email became a Mirror connection, and was quickly turning into love within a couple of weeks—even though we had never actually met."
—Jonathan, on encountering his first Mirror

In the film *The Matrix Revolutions*, the character Merovingian says, "It is remarkable how similar the pattern of love is to the pattern of insanity." Possibly he would have said the same to Jonathan as he headed to his first date with Dawn, 3,000 miles and 8 states to east. That's right. John traveled to his first date with Dawn on a plane! As the plane landed, Jonathan distinctly recalls thinking, "What the hell am I doing here?"

Deep inside, however, Jonathan knew the answer. Connection! His connection with Dawn was incredibly strong. Connection made it possible for him to believe and broke through his walls of doubt. Connection gave him confidence in the potential of their relationship. Connection made their love real, bonded their hearts together, and made a 3,000 mile first date the only reasonable course.

The power of connection makes the impossible seem possible. Eclipsing the amazing, beyond profound, more than you dare imagine—it is more than a dream can hold. The power grabs you when you least expect it and vaults you onto a plane (sometimes a jet plane) of connection beyond anything you've ever thought possible.

Easy, Meaningful, and Connected Dates

"He started writing me last Thursday. When we met last night in the aisle at Whole Foods, I had no expectations. In fact I thought it was going to be a quick meet and that would be that. We ended up going to Sushi and then spent six hours (until 3 am) in his car in the parking lot! Definitely Mirroring in a very HUGE way. Time will tell, but we are already very bonded." —Renee: 1 date

The ease of the connection is remarkable. Once connection is found, dates are filled with discovery and discussion on topics that are meaningful to you at your core. Superficial groping-for-a-common-interest-to-get-this-thing-off-the-ground is replaced with deep, meaningful conversation. It is common for Mirror dates to continue nonstop for hours.

Illuminates Potential

"And now I am no longer waiting. Your kisses, hugs and voice are the comfort for which I've always yearned. Your heart and soul touch me in the deepest places—places only you can touch. I am no longer waiting for someone to understand me, to nurture my love in warmth, to meet me in everything that I am. My dreams pale. I can see our future, who we are together, so clearly. We were meant to be." —Tom: 3 weeks

Potential is the sum of possibilities in any given pairing. Within openness and connection we can see the mixing of Mirror Elements (communication, compatibility, chemistry, etc) between two people. We can observe the results of the pairing and begin to extrapolate the ultimate potential of the relationship.

Validation

"The need I have for affection is so strong. It is not a pathetic insecure need. It is who I am. I feel empty without it. I used to think there was something wrong with me, that I had this strong desire for physical touch, intimate conversation, until I met you. Maybe, that is why you were brought into my life. I just wanted you to know in the little time I've known you, you have impacted my life greatly." —Heidi: 5 dates

The power of connection validates the deepest parts of us, places we think no one can or ever will ever understand. Yet, here, at this very moment, right in front of you is someone who understands and reflects you *precisely*. Where others may have made us feel apart, different, or alone, the Mirror Effect brings validation to the very essence of *who we are*. This is what the soul seeks. To be met—to have our lives, thoughts, feelings understood and validated. These are *emotional* Mirrors.

Shared life experiences are responsible for this unique empathic connection—a connection that allows us to personally identify with each other. Fear cannot stand against a connection this powerful. Walls, built strong with bricks of pain and anguish, are pierced in the same way the sun cuts through the night. We learn that we are not different—not alone—and that brings deep comfort and peace.

Surrendering to Connection

"When I finally let it just flow, I felt you inside me, as if your soul was one with mine. An understanding that needs no words. I am on my way home in so many ways."—Theresa: 23 days

The power of connection can bring a tsunami of fears—the fear of having such a match, the fear of losing it, the fear that we might be wrong, the fear that it might change, the fear that it might not last.

Surrender is the antidote to fear. Surrendering to the connection liberates the heart and makes us the best of everything we can be. Surrender allows the Mirror relationship to develop naturally, albeit very quickly. With a history of traditional dating, there may be resistance; however, surrender is best way to use the Mirror Effect to find a Magical Match.

TIPS FOR DISCOVERING CONNECTION

Armed with a head full of new concepts and paradigms, all that remains is to set the stage for finding connection. Remember, just being in the same place and sharing openly and honestly, a connection will be established, if there is one to be found. Beyond that, all you need are a few dating tips:

Select a quiet place for first dates

Dating is about uncovering connection and discovering potential; setting the environment for that to happen is crucial. I always ensure that the first dates are in a setting that is conducive to intimate discussions. Coffee shops tend to be noisy with all the drinks being made and table conversations going on. A nice, quiet restaurant is a better choice. Perhaps a picnic in a quiet corner of a park. Somewhere that the two of you feel safe to open up without distractions.

Be transparent

When I was dating, I always planned on being transparent—completely open, honest and genuine. There is no question I wouldn't answer, no subject taboo. I made it a point to let my date see through me—to touch my heart and soul. Transparency is how I ensured no connection went undiscovered.

The quickest, best way is to establish trust is to approach with a completely open, vulnerable heart.

Be vulnerable

I also practiced *extreme* vulnerability. I was there, at a date, having profiled, filtered, and measured. I *believed* that a Mirror was sitting in front of me. What would be accomplished if I waded in tentatively? What would happen if I did the exact opposite? "Here—this is my heart and it's yours to hold for as long as we're together. Take care; it is fragile, it can be hurt—and I give it willingly."

Instead of seeing my caution, my dates felt my openness—vulnerability—willingness to risk. She could sense the truth and my genuine character. It's very disarming when a woman's intuition tells her that a man is trustworthy and safe. She almost subconsciously discards her apprehension, and as she does, walls begin to crumble—not brick by brick, but in massive chunks. The transformation is both visible and palpable. As walls are replaced with trust, the full, true person emerges. Unfettered by fear, hearts, souls, and minds begin a journey of mutual discovery.

Vulnerability enables deep connection. The potential of *everything* we can be together lies within connection.

Come out from behind your walls. Be authentic, unguarded. Openly share the essence of who you are in order to allow the connection, if any, to be found.

The simple dating tips will create better dates and connections. What type of connection depends upon the level of Mirroring between daters. In a typical date, you can anticipate experiencing one of three levels of connection:

- Typical date: Nice person, but nothing in common—no connection. The more accurate and open your Mirror Profile, the fewer unconnected dates you should encounter.

- A new friend: A great connection and a pleasurable date, but not particularly relationship material, no overwhelming gravity or connection.
- A Mirror: An amazing connection on too many levels to be believable. A surreal experience of connection and gravity.

You will know when you have met a Mirror when you experience the following:

- You instantly recognize yourself within them.
- The connection is *obvious*. You feel at peace, overjoyed—surreal, but also grounded.
- The gravity of the connection is palpable, deep.
- The feeling of coming home—or that you have known your date forever—is present.
- You feel compelled to move forward.

But don't worry for a second if:

- You share openly and don't find a connection. There is nothing wrong with that. Remember, Mirrors are searching for a pre-existing connection. Not finding one means that it never existed. If your date walks away, it wasn't right anyway.
- You know that you've found a Mirror, but your Mirror date doesn't completely understand or lean in right away. Remember Judy's first response after falling in love on the (second) first date. *"Speechless sums it up perfectly...and have you seen my sunglasses?"* is not exactly the message you'd expect, but it's understandable given the suddenness.

CONVERTING SKEPTICS

"When I first met Troy in 2008, I liked him very much. We went on few dates and had a great time. He quickly let me know he was looking for a Mirror and what that meant for him. I was skeptical but amused. What was the harm? He was adorable, romantic, fun and smart. So what if he had this quirky, bizarre idea?"—Judy, Sept. 2010

Like Judy, almost everyone starts out as skeptic when they first learn about Mirroring. That's perfectly normal when presented with a paradigm that flies in the face of everything promulgated as relationship truth. Often though, what we believe to be the truth ends up being something different. After all, the Earth *is* flat, yes?

Don't confuse prevailing wisdom with *truth*.

The truth about Mirror pairings can be found in the words of Jonathan, Renee, Tom, Heidi, Theresa, and Judy. The Power of Connection is unique, an awesome force that shifts lives in moments without counselors or self-help. The truth is that the Mirror Effect validates and heals, dissolves walls and fears. The truth is that, through the Power of Connection, it is possible to find a more powerful love than you ever thought possible.

The Mirror connection is a *force*—palpable, unconditional, soul deep.

There are no skeptics in the warm light of *that* divine love.

"The minute I heard my first love story, I started looking for you, not knowing how blind that was. Lovers don't finally meet somewhere. They're in each other all along."
—Rumi, *The Illuminated Rumi*

Key Concepts

- It's not about building connection, but discovering if one already exists.
- Openness and transparency are the paths to discovering connection.
- Dating is about discovering the potential within any given pairing.
- Openness, coupled with the gravity of connection, allows an exploration of the depth and breadth of a pairing.
- Connection breaks through walls and fears in the most amazing way.
- The Mirror connection is astonishing. It approaches the surreal. Mirror connection transforms lives *profoundly*.
- Skeptics are those who have yet to experience the Mirror connection for themselves.

Mirror Effect Law

- The Mirror connection is an undeniable, incredible force.

Steps Towards Your Magical Match

- Discover the *full* potential of each date by being genuine, authentic, honest, transparent, and expressive with your feelings. Be open to being hurt, willing to lose, and expect to win.
- Follow the connection. Only invest time and effort with dates with whom you share a deep connection.
- Surrender to connection. Go with whatever feels right. Don't let your head get in the way.
- If you're not finding enough connections, reevaluate your Profile. It may need modification before you try again.
- Don't try to control the connection or flow of the relationship. Doing so disrupts the natural pattern of the Mirror Effect.

- Don't be an unconscious Picker. Do not continue to date poor Mirrors.

Is My Date a Mirror?

- Is this person in some ways exactly like you? Do you feel genuinely, deeply amazed how much you are alike? Do they feel like a copy of you?
- Does this connection give you a calming peace that you have not previously known?
- Does it just seem obvious that this is a relationship?
- Do you feel like you have known this person for much longer than you actually have? Is there a feeling like you've come home?
- Do you feel a deep connection? A gravity of being pulled into something deep and wonderful about this person?
- Does this pairing pull out the very best in you?
- Do you share some strong similar life experiences?
- Do you tend to think alike? Do you share the same perspectives and outlooks on life, love, politics, work, etc?
- When you speak, do you feel like you need to explain your thoughts or are they understood without you having to explain (especially when they aren't precisely clear or well formed)?
- Is it easy to be together? Can you talk easily for hours and hours? Is this supremely comfortable?
- Do you feel chemistry? Good energy, but not completely bouncing off the walls energy—something different. A chemistry that is also grounded, deep, peaceful.
- Does the connection feel a little overwhelming?
- Deep inside we always really know. What does your heart tell you?

11

MY BROKEN PICKER

MY BROKEN PICKER

Judy Tells Her Story

What I know from being a woman is that shopping is an art. You don't just go to the store and pick out the perfect outfit. You must *learn* to shop—and there is much more to this art form than meets the eye. You must know who you are, what styles you are comfortable with, what looks good on your particular body, and what colors suit you best. And most importantly, it takes time and great discernment to find a perfect fit and to settle for nothing less.

I know because I have brought home many misfit shoes, shirts and sweaters over the years. Why? Because I didn't have a clear understanding of exactly what best suited me and I didn't have a method to ensure that I didn't buy an outfit that really wouldn't work for me.

Clothes or men, shopping is shopping—and my less than stellar aptitude for clothes shopping directly correlated to my lack of success in shopping for men. Haphazard at best, my relationships were to a great degree chosen unconsciously and by chance. Not having ever witnessed or experienced close, loving, intimate relationships, I never saw anything I wanted to emulate. As a result, I didn't believe that a loving, deeply-connected, intimate relationship was possible at all—and certainly not possible for me. So my relationships always followed the same pattern:

- They would start out great and then slowly, over the first few months to a year, I would find areas where our differences caused struggle and strife. There would be obvious areas of discord.
- I would find aspects of my partner I did not like and I would not like who I became with my partner.
- I would go into denial, ignoring the signs and symptoms. I'd leave my proverbial head in the sand for as long as possible.
- When I just couldn't deny it any longer, I would try to fix the issue. I always believed that our problems must be due to miscommunication or a lack of understanding between us.
- When this didn't work, I would blame myself and try to fix me. If I were only more patient, loving and caring, it would all be all right.
- As none of these strategies ever worked for me, I would finally admit that he wasn't the right partner and break it off. And then I'd repeat the same thing all over again.

And that's how it was with every man I ever dated: Wet, wash, rinse, repeat. Don't get me wrong; all of the men I brought home over the years had wonderful characteristics, but in the end none of them really fit me just right. I was always going 'round the dating wheel.

Since I didn't have the inclination to marry or have children, this repeated pattern did not hinder me from any specific life goal, but it also did not result in a deeply loving, connected, lasting relationship—the one thing that was really my heart's deepest desire. And after going through this cycle over and over again, I knew that if I continued with my pattern, I would be 70 and still dating.

My second first date with Troy changed everything. Our immediate connection was a surprise. Over dinner, we had a deep conversation. I felt at one with him, like we already knew each other and the date was just a formality. The depth and intensity of our connection left me speechless and in shock. I had had many relationships, many first dates and many times when I felt giddy, excited, immediately in love—"Wow, this is the guy." But with Troy, things were different. Our connection—from that moment on—felt calm and peaceful and grounded.

I remember sitting on my couch after our first date realizing I was in love with him and that was that. However fast and odd it seemed, I decided to just let it be what it was. It was like someone telling you the sky is blue. You just say yes, that's true. It just was.

Still, even though our relationship was different, I expected my habitual pattern with relationships to repeat. But that didn't happen with Troy. Instead, something amazing happened. As we moved through our days, it became clear to me that the way we processed information, our attitudes and outlook on life was almost identical. It made our time together easy and fun; there was no conflict, no misunderstanding—we were just free to enjoy each other and life together. What's more, I had a tendency to protect my soft underbelly—my tender, compassionate heart—with an outer shell of tough, independent, strong woman. But with Troy I didn't need this. I softened. And not just with him, but with life in general. I felt truly seen and understood by Troy and, with that gift, I was able to relax fully, to be more of *me*.

Despite these major differences between my previous relationships and my relationship with Troy, in my head, I still doubted it would last. Deep inside I didn't believe it could. I had never been in a relationship that didn't have some downside. My past relationships had always required compromise and left me feeling that something was missing, but with Troy, each time we faced a situation that could have taken us down—or where we could have found an irreconcilable difference—we found instead that we understood and agreed with the other's perspective and interpretation of life.

Each time this happened, I realized this was due to an aspect inside of us that mirrored each other so well. Because we were so similar inside, we lived our lives and wanted to express ourselves similarly on the outside. As time passed, our days continued to be filled with the deepest, most intimate, heartfelt, amazing love I have ever experienced. Secretly, I always thought this kind of love existed—out there somewhere—maybe for other people—but now finally it was happening to me. To us. This love—the love I'd always wanted—was mine.

What I've come to understand is that learning how to shop is a lot easier than I thought it would be. First and foremost you need to know it is possible and set your mark on "The One." You need to be committed to getting the love you want to the point of obsession, and not settle for less, even if it is far beyond anything you have known previously. You need to know your deepest essence, those innate qualities that make you *you*, and hardest of all, when you find someone who looks really close, but there is one thing that doesn't fit, don't buy him!

My relationship with Troy trained my broken picker. After being with my Mirror, I can no longer can imagine doing with anything less. Nothing but a Magical Match will ever do again.

"Let yourself be drawn by the stronger pull of that which you truly love." —Rumi

STEP 4 - SELECTION

A good match is more than good love; a great match is more than great love

Falling in love is easy. Even the village idiot can fall in love. Any given blend of pheromones and attraction can create the "I'm in love" euphoria. And that's how it always starts.

But how can you discern fit through the fog of love? Clairvoyance? If the village idiot were clairvoyant he wouldn't be the village idiot! And that's what you become when you fall in love without a dating strategy. No sage plan, no equation, no process, no filter—just show up for a date and let love's chips fall where they may. The hard, cold truth?

Being in love is the lowest common denominator of all selection criteria.

Jessie met Zack, her first boyfriend, when she was 19. It was a typical boy meets girl story—well, except that it was a blind date. They met, dated, enjoyed each other, and eventually married. Certainly there was attraction, though now, 15 years later, it is difficult for Jessie to precisely recall the chemistry that initially captured them. She does, however, recall problems from the outset. Zack had jealousy issues. Zack's anger flared every time a man got near her. Jessie continued forward, ignorant of the warning signs. Her formative years had been spent constantly moving, *and* she was a late bloomer. This combination left her completely inexperienced and unprepared for a relationship. Even worse, what does *any* 19-year-old know about life or life partners?

Jessie had made a decision, rather blindly in retrospect, to begin what she assumed would be a lifetime marriage. It lasted 15 years—some happy, some sad, many tears, and too much effort.

Why did Jessie select Zack? Certainly she was in love at the time. She thought that just by being with her, Zack would eventually change. Isn't that the way love is supposed to work? We learn our partners—love their strengths, forgive their faults. Love conquers all. I can fix this—fix him—fix everything. Compromise is necessary. We can work it out. (Feel free to enlist your own misguided notions).

But Jessie was wrong. Her marriage to Zack was wrong. They were wrong for each other.

LOVE BEFORE MATCH –
THE SLIPPERY DOWNHILL SLOPE

Without training, what algorithm do we employ to help us with this monumental leap? Did we marry him because he has money? Or her because she has large breasts? Maybe the sex is otherworldly. Still, it's annoyingly irritating when he repeatedly takes phone calls during dinner. "He's important; he has to take those calls," she tells her guests. "I don't mind. I love him and that's what really counts!"—as if *love* itself portends a successful pairing. Boy, if only that equation worked elsewhere: I'm certain I was in love with a chocolate chip cookie last night, but it turned out to be just an oral fling.

Cookies or marriage, our selection criterion is *love*. Left to our own devices, selection is driven largely by pheromones and attraction. We meet, feel some connection and attraction, and fall forward into love. It's a natural pattern, one that is at the base of almost every modern relationship. But when all of the varnish is stripped away, the truth becomes obvious; hidden within this seemingly benign pattern is an insidious progression that subverts the Picker's ability to properly select.

It takes longer for matching to be revealed than it does to fall in love!

In what is probably a biological race to sustain the species, love outruns the desire for high compatibility and leaves in its wake a couple that is in love, but not highly compatible. Instead of using dating to discern match, we slip love-dumb downhill into relationship. Once invested in love, mismatches go unchecked as the relationship marches forward, a million-minute countdown to marriage. The intervening countdown gives chance that a glimmer of clairvoyance will pierce the fog; but, even being able to finally recognize incompatibility, the Picker, ensnared by biology, often selects marriage rather than to begin again with a better match.

A slippery downhill slope indeed.

TRADITIONAL SELECTION – ALL THINGS NOT EQUAL

The reason traditional selection fails is that we arrive at a date without a plan to test a predetermined list of characteristics; the first date becomes a search for chemistry and *any* common matching trait that might lead to a deeper connection. This progression eventually leads us to *first* fall in love and *then* make a mindless, de facto selection.

Let's illustrate how this progression occurs by examining Jill, a traditional dater, and her possible candidates: Jim, Xavier, and Silas. Jill's communication with each has revolved around her mostly superficial, traditional profile, and after several emails, she's reached a place where she would like to meet each of them.

Up first is Jim. When Jill meets Jim she instantly notices a lack of attraction. For most, like Jill, attraction is an element that carries a high value—and there's nothing wrong with that. It's just part of her personality type. As the evening progresses she discovers:

- They share good logistics
    - Jim lives very close to her.
    - They both have no children.

- They share similar perspectives
    - They both believe in the giving to the downtrodden.
    - They both feel life is too short to hold grudges.

- They seem pretty compatible
    - They share many values and beliefs.
    - They are both clean and organized.

Now, if we were to graph her match to Jim, it would look something like this:

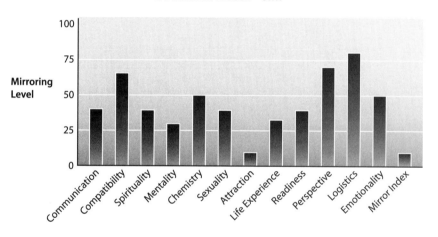

Analyzing Jill's match with Jim, most of the traits are lowly matched, except for Perspective and Logistics. Other than those things, there isn't much of a match. Her Mirror Index (a calculation based upon each of the individual traits) with Jim is low—about 15.

Then Jill meets Xavier and, again, no attraction (darn!); he just doesn't fit her predilection for tall, lean men. Again, though, she encounters a couple of stronger elements during the date.

- Logistics
  - -He lives and works fairly close to her.
  - -He has one child that doesn't live at home.
  - -They both make about the same amount of money.

- Chemistry
  - -There was a little bit of spark—their conversation flowed pretty well

Traditional Match – Xavier

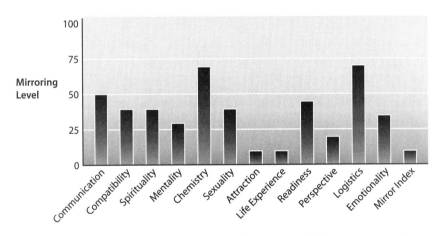

Because he isn't her attraction predilection, Jill has just one date with Xavier. Next up? Silas!

Jill meets Silas. Silas is tall, lean, and handsome. Attraction, sweet attraction! Their dates go quite well. Jill finds good matching with Silas on:

- Logistics
  - -They live and work close to each other.
  - -Both financially sound.
  - -Neither has children.

- Perspective
  - -They share a perspective on life's priorities.

- Chemistry
  - -There is a great spark. They never stop laughing.

- Attraction
  - -They are each other's perfect predilection.

Traditional Match – Silas

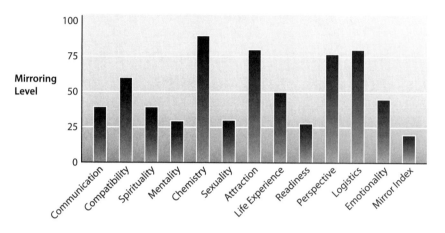

With Chemistry and Attraction, biology provides a good spark, and higher matching Perspective and Logistics add to the pairing potential. In combination, these traits create enough of a connection to provide an incentive to continue dating. As Jill and Silas continue dating, she hopes that the emotional connection will grow, and that love will blossom.

In terms of selection:

- Jill discards Xavier and Jim due to a lack of matching.
- Jill selects to go forward with Silas, primarily on just *four* matching traits.

But the mismatching traits that Jill ignores are much more important than those that match. Traits such as emotionality, mentality, and spirituality are very likely to be points of friction in this relationship, and the problems will multiply because their communication, the ability to understand each other, is low as well. Nevertheless, because they are attracted and lonely, they continue forward together and eventually fall in love.

In this love-before-match relationship, critical relational elements are ignored when the selection decision is cast. *Rather than disqualifying Silas for relationship, love-before-match creates an environment where a highly mismatched partner is perceived as having marriage potential.*

MIRROR SELECTION – ALL THINGS BEING EQUAL

We need a new dating regimen that liberates us from the failed, old way of dating. If the natural biological progression is to fall forward into mismatched love, the process of selection must begin *before* the first date. The design must consider critical elements beyond love: communication, mentality, spirituality, sexuality, and logistics, to name just a few. The methodology must also educate the Picker to recognize the minutest mismatches and penetrate love's biological fog. Finally, a renewed confidence must accompany the Picker on the journey towards selecting a life partner.

The Mirror Effect allows us to approach selection differently. A completely opposite paradigm than *traditional* matching, Mirroring draws forward potential candidates with highly similar compatibility traits *across the board,* creating a recognizable fingerprint for finding potential Mirrors.

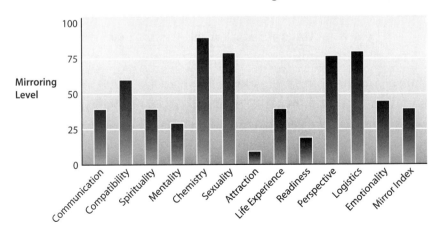

Traditional Matching

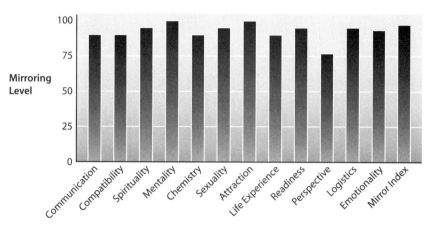

Mirror Pairing

Mirroring Level

When you look at the charts above, what do you notice?

In the *Traditional Matching* chart, we look for what's the *same*. The mind notes the high points: Chemistry, Sexuality, and Attraction are all high in the traditional matching chart.

In the Mirror Pairing chart, the mind pinpoints the *low* characteristics—what's *different*—instead. Because everything is highly matching, the nature of the fingerprint compels us to recognize the mirror chart's dip at Life Perspective. Even more amazing, *the mind focuses on the minuscule differences* for communication, compatibility, and chemistry, which, in reality, are all scores of **90**!

The same phenomenon that happens on paper occurs in real life. *The Mirror Effect spontaneously shifts our concentration to the characteristics that are not matched.* We become more aware of the mismatches without even trying. In fact, the experienced Mirror dater *naturally* focuses on the pairing mismatches. In essence, match-before-love makes us picky! It's just another self-correcting Mirror Effect element.

Mirroring transforms the blind expedition for matching into a precise analysis of each individual relationship element.

Once again let's examine three potential pairings, this time for Mirror dater Tyler. Tyler's Mirror Profile has filtered Valeria, Kate, and Yuki from the dating pool. After dating each of them, Tyler has charted the results of their pairings.

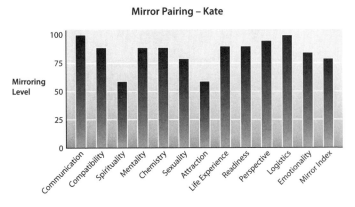

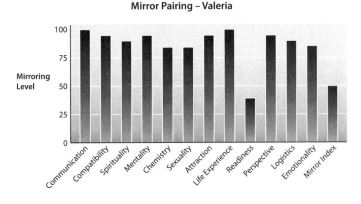

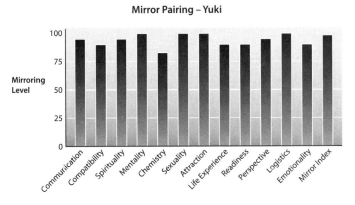

- With Kate, Spirituality and Attraction are the standout elements.
- With Valeria, the much lower ranking Readiness predominates the fingerprint.
- Even with Yuki, where every other element is 90 or better, the miniscule dip in Chemistry (80) is evident.

Do you see how element *deficits* predominate the characteristics? Tyler does. He is able to know that Valeria's walls are not likely to fall soon and that his and Kate's spirituality is mismatched. Because John naturally begins to see what's missing in these pairings, he is better able to select Yuki, a Mirror that has real potential as a Magical Match. By beginning with matching criteria, the Mirror Effect creates a recognizable fingerprint for finding and measuring potential Mirrors.

PURE, UNOBSCURED CLARITY

When we Mirror date, we tend to encounter people who are highly matched, but have one or two lower matching traits (like Valeria and Kate). These experiences are a gift, an opportunity to share a date with someone who has everything mirrored except mentality, for instance. Clarity emerges as we experience the lacking mentality characteristics in *isolation*; a telling pothole in an otherwise perfect street. We get to see what happens when our Mirror doesn't think like us or communicate in the same way we do. Because every other characteristic is highly matched, we know that what is not working is due to a specific lowly matched characteristic. As we date in a pool of Mirrors, we have the unique opportunity to see and experience each characteristic and come to understand how that particular trait affects us in a relationship.

With a little experience, Mirror daters sensitize and naturally begin to discern, compare, and contrast the various types and levels of matching that works for them: "That guy worked really well—communication, compatibility, and spirituality, but there just wasn't enough matching mentality—we just thought a little too differently".

When was the last time you dissected a date so precisely? Clarity. Pure clarity.

Amazingly, the Picker begins to function, even through the fog of love, as the mind, once subjugated to biology, fixates upon a blemish, unable to ignore its existence. Daters no longer blindly explore or fall forward. Instead they are compelled to investigate, weigh, and decide. Confusion becomes confidence, clarity splits the fog, biology transforms into true selection. Mirrors Matchers quickly learn to discern the strongest pairings while simultaneously identifying the smallest mismatches. Now *that's* selection!

THE PERILS IN SELECTION
Inequality Breeds Resentment

Inequity in relationships can produce difficulties, even for Mirrors. He is 50; she is 28. She is a movie star, he is a mechanic, and, as such, she makes an 8-figure salary; he makes $40,000 a year. All of these situations create areas where jealously, insecurity, or feelings of inadequacy might arise to create relational misunderstandings.

Mirror relationships tend to be better when there is equality. Financial, educational, status, or other inequalities can unbalance Mirror relationships, putting them at risk of falling apart.

Balance is everything in a Mirror relationship and is a critical component in finding a Magical Match.

The Near Miss

The Near Miss is a Mirror who doesn't turn out to be a Magical Match. Whether it is logistics, walls, readiness, mismatching—

whatever the block(s)—the near miss is close, but just not quite there. A two-edged sword, soul connection creates a bond in both perfect and near-perfect pairings. In order to find your Magical Match, *you must learn to encounter immense gravity and still be able to let go of Mirrors who are maddeningly close, but just beyond your reach.*

Chasing Potential

With Mirroring, we begin to be able to predict the outcome of our Mirror pairings. As each of your Mirrors is highly similar, the relationship elements you experience will become familiar. If all of your Mirrors have a tender, deep quality (because you are tender and deep), after a while you begin to be able to easily sense those qualities in your dates. But what if you meet someone whom you can absolutely distinguish as a Mirror, but she has a wall of fear around opening her heart? Your mind tells you that everything about her is perfect: she is your Magical Match—except for this one thing.

This is a place to be very careful. In reality, this ideal woman with the guarded heart is not your Magical Match. She has *potential* as a Magical Match, but the Mirror cannot be fully reflective, the pairing fully revealed, until she moves beyond her wall of fear.

The danger in this circumstance is *chasing potential.* The inclination is to perform the extraordinary in attempts to help her through her wall. *If I can just be more vulnerable and loving and open, she'll move past her fear. I know she can do it. She's right there. She is my Magical Match, there's just this one thing.* In the midst of the gravity of your pairing, it is incredibly easy to chase potential. But if the wall does not quickly fall, she becomes a near miss—a Mirror that cannot be your Magical Match.

The Dead Zone

The Dead Zone is a place of extreme indecision or difficulty. It occurs when the sum of all the positive traits overrides just one severely mismatched trait. Maybe a Mirror pairing is superlative, except that he has a much higher libido. In every other way, their relationship is off-the-charts, but this one thing is frequently in the way. Neither partner can stand the thought of releasing this otherwise amazing relationship, and at the same time, this one crucial mismatch flares to create severe unrest and work.

There are no Magical Matches in The Dead Zone, only near misses.

Remember, If It's Work, It's Wrong

Almost everything works. However, *almost* is not enough. Instead of living a loving existence, significant time is spent in struggling to force the broken, mismatched relationship bits into submission. The mismatched Mirror daters persist because the fatally flawed relationship is still the best they've ever had—by far.

On the path to finding your Magical Match, mismatched or misbalanced couples must learn to let go and start again. But this is much easier said than done. In theory, you might see the rationale. But in reality...? It's wrenching. Letting go of relationships that are balanced across 95% of the elements is incredibly difficult. However, that missing 5% will invariably and insidiously play against the rest. The smallest lack of attraction affects the depth of lovemaking, the slightest incompatibility unsettles what would otherwise be the deepest connection.

When Do I Stop Looking?

Knowing when you've met your Magical Match can be a bit difficult, especially if you've known multiple Mirrors. Comparing and contrasting each Mirror relationship does not really provide complete insight. Paradoxically, if you're more focused on what is wrong than what is right, then at least you're in the Mirror frame of mind.

Read over the "Is My Date a Mirror?" questions on page 103 to ascertain if your relationship has all or most of the Mirror elements. Consider the graph of Elements earlier in this chapter and take an honest look at the lowest-level characteristics are in your pairing. Ensure you aren't in a Dead Zone.

If you're feeling crazy happy and well met, and there are no caveats or work or significant compromises, then it is probably time to stop looking.

MY EXPERIENCE WITH SELECTION

Being the first in anything can be difficult, especially when you're breaking new ground. For me, the path towards the goal was fraught with hazards and prone to failures as I learned to recognize what worked and what didn't. These difficulties multiplied exponentially because the equation components were as intangible as love and as complex as relationships.

To make matters even more challenging, my personality type made it harder to find Judy. I describe my personality type as "mid-brainer." Whereas most people are predominately either intellectual or emotional, a mid-brainer is equally head *and* heart; we can shift between the two almost instantaneously. As you might imagine, with a personality type that is both rare and at the extremes, finding a true Mirror is nearly as difficult as hitting the lottery. In fact, it wasn't until I amended my original profile that I started to attract those more aligned with my mid-brainer type:

A true mid-brainer—both intellectual and spiritual. I can write music as well as a patent, I am romantic and a realist, cerebral and emotional. Words said most about me: sweet; romantic; cute, sometimes handsome; affectionate, gentleman; integrity; character, passionate, sensual.

And that is the beauty of Online Dating—it's capacity to be used as a precision tool. Even with significant obstacles, in the three years that I employed my Mirror Profile, I met *six* Mirrors, an average of about one every six months! That is an astounding statistic; especially given that I only had about 30 first dates (the Mirror Process *really* does work). Of my six Mirror relationships:

- One wasn't ready for the intensity of a Mirror relationship.
- In two relationships, I had issues with a lack of attraction.
  -The connection in both was *incredibly* strong, so the lack of attraction created a Dead Zone. Dead Zones are, well, deadly.
- One had logistical issues over which I had no control.
- One just wasn't a mid-brainer.
- One was just right—and that was Judy!

Certainly, I made errors in selection as I learned about the intricacies of the Mirror Effect, errors I would avoid now:

- For me, and those who share my personality type, attraction is a key relationship element. I would never again select for relationship where attraction was weak, regardless of the gravitational pull.
- I would look at logistics with a much more critical eye.
- I would never chase potential again (and never did).

These were hard fought, heartbreaking lessons for both me and my Mirrors; ones I hope this book will help you avoid. Still, in all likelihood, you will know more than one Mirror before making a life-partner selection. It may sound like a curse, but it is really a gift. The experience of multiple Mirrors is a richly detailed exploration in the subtleties of pairing and Mirror relationships. The more Mirrors you come to know, the better your filter becomes. Your Picker attunes, revealing not just whether characteristics are matching, but their *level* of match or mismatch. The more Mirrors you meet, the more your own personal selection criteria becomes clear and well defined. And because you have met more than one Mirror, you grow more confident, knowing that you can create lightning again, if needed.

Considering all things, it is pretty amazing that I went from absolute zero to finding my Magical Match in three years. I suspect that as we learn and experience more in the Mirror realm, it will be possible to go even faster; maybe *much* faster. The future will tell.

Key Concepts:
- Love is the lowest common denominator of all selection criteria.
- Love-before-match is the path to traditional, mismatched relationships.
- Match-before-love creates an environment where the Picker learns to select properly.
- When presented with Mirrors, and their highly-matching trait levels, the mind naturally focuses on the deficient elements—on *what's missing*. The effect is so powerful that it is possible to select even through the fog of attraction and sex.
- Balance is a key to successful Mirror pairings.

Mirror Effect Laws:
- There are no Magical Matches in The Dead Zone.

Steps Towards Your Magical Match
- Avoid love-before-match—the insidious progression that leads to mismatched relationships.
- Be aware and actively observe all relationship characteristics, not just love. Be an intelligent Picker and select a superlative *pairing*!

- Remember to mind your Tango. Match your partner's steps and frame. Don't constantly push in or lean out.
- Don't be the village idiot; use a dating plan!
- Don't chase potential.
- Don't ignore what isn't matching. If the absence or weakness of a particular characteristic causes friction or work, it's probably time to let go and start over again. Remember, you have more than one Mirror. You can do this again.

13

STEP 5 - LETTING GO

"Train yourself to let go of everything you fear to lose."
–Yoda

I know firsthand the crushing pain of losing a Mirror relationship...

In the third month of my first Mirror relationship, Helen began to withdraw. A project at work filled her schedule to the point where she didn't have time for us. But there was something deeper going on. I noticed that she had begun to withdraw emotionally as well. A lifetime of pain and suffering left her unprepared for the speed and intensity of our Mirroring. Even though we had been engaged for two months and were discussing a wedding, I had yet to be invited to her house because she had such a strong distrust of men.

I put forth a Herculean effort to make the relationship safe for her: the engagement, listening, reassuring, connection, attention, affection, presence—all in the extreme, all to help her feel safe. I was in deep. For me, her potential as my Magical Match was obvious and compelling. I could see and feel it. If I could only do enough, be patient enough, try a little harder, then maybe she would see it as well—maybe she would stretch past her obstacles.

Instead, Helen's unresolved issues became re-elevated walls, and she hit them hard. She pulled away and it nearly killed me. This was the relationship I had waited an entire lifetime to have and it was slipping away. When she hit the wall, it set off my own liquefaction, forcing my fears to the surface. I leaned in; she leaned out. The chain of events between us set off an unrecoverable Death Spiral. Our Mirror relationship crashed spectacularly into an exploding heap.

Weaknesses, walls, chasing potential, an unbalanced tango, and an undeclared Death Spiral. I had made every mistake possible. The gravity of our connection was so great that I had been blinded. Had I known then what I know now, I would have let go of the relationship much sooner.

Of all the steps in the Mirroring Process, *Letting Go* is unerringly the most difficult. Because in order to understand the full potential of a Mirror pairing, the heart must vulnerably step forward and breathe in each connection. Inhaling deeply, hearts, minds, and souls bind with a force known only by a fortunate few. Paradoxically, in the midst of overwhelming gravity, we must reserve the ability to release the relationship, if necessary. Letting go of something deeper than you've ever known, all the while believing that someone even better is out there, requires a leap of faith and determination.

Unfortunately, no profile can assess a date's level of readiness, and no filter can screen every Mirror's weaknesses. Even in a brave new world where we consciously choose Mirrors, those damaged by life cannot be systematically screened, and neither can the vagaries of love and emotion be discounted. Regardless of how careful, how observant, how diligent we are, the Mirroring Process attracts both near misses *and* our Magical Match. Separating the two requires that we connect equally to each Mirror—which means having the willingness to bond and express deeply—*as part of the selection process*. We need to understand that our connection to near misses—the *almost* Magical Match—is going to be incredibly strong. In anticipation, we *must* develop an equalizing skill that enables us, in fact, compels us, to let go. We need a letting go methodology.

TALBOT'S MOTTO: "SHOOT THE STRAGGLERS, CARRY THE WOUNDED, HURDLE THE DEAD"

Google. No definition or explanation is necessary. Their campus is swimming in more Ph.D.s than fish in a trout farm. But, what the heck does Google have to do with relationships (other than as a tool for searching for online dating sites)?

One of Google's business strategies is to harvest ideas for new products from all those brilliant minds. Even flush with great concepts, Google understands that not every attempted product will succeed. With finite resources and seemingly infinite ideas, it's challenging to launch new products, sustain successful projects, and simultaneously invest in improving products that are not making the grade.

So how has Google succeeded? "Fail Fast" is their answer. "Fail Fast" is a Google-developed discipline to terminate projects that are not working. Rather than endlessly tweak, Google shoots the stragglers and hurdles the dead, killing projects that aren't distinctly successful. With great prejudice towards efficiency, Fail Fast culls the unsuccessful in favor of focusing on winning combinations. As a tactic, Fail Fast forces potential into either culmination or termination.

Letting Go in the Mirror realm is a Fail Fast philosophy. Unlike traditional relationships that depend upon a long ramp time, Mirror relationships come pre-matched. What we need to discover are any potential weaknesses and the levels of Mirroring. We need to understand where our Mirrors are weak, if there are walls, and how well—or poorly—the Mirroring is balanced. Because Mirrors are already connected, it doesn't take long to discover what we need to know. Within the Mirror relationship pattern, this should certainly occur within 4 months at the very far edge, usually much faster if we're actually paying attention, and not deluding ourselves with protracted traditional-think. Like Google, we have limited time and resources. We *need* these relationships to either culminate or terminate. It's the only way we can reach our ultimate goal of finding a Magical Match with speed, certainty, and confidence.

BUT HOW CAN I GIVE UP THE BEST RELATIONSHIP I'VE EVER HAD?!

Even as you recognize the need to let go, the struggle to do so can be an overwhelming mental battle. You may find yourself torn with an intensity that you've never encountered before. *I love her; I have to let her go. I need her, but it's not working. I love her, but I can do better* can become a constant soundtrack in your head. It's the most extreme game of emotional ping-pong you can imagine—one second you're letting go and ten seconds later, you're not. The self-correcting nature of the Mirror Effect causes you to see the flaws in the relationship and, at the same time, the gravity keeps you locked in orbit.

Try not to worry too much about this extremely torn state. Eventually, the strength of the Let Go response will overcome the magnetic pull of the relationship. When that occurs, it will be a little easier to let go. Until then, have an open dialogue about what's happening for you. Continue with the relationship until you're ready to let it go.

But beware. Once you finally decide to end the relationship, the Spin Cycle can kick in. Every day you promise yourself you'll give up caffeine, yet somehow that tall quadruple skinny half-soy extra-foamy Latte keeps finding its way into your hand, and in the same way, you find yourself repeatedly returning to that near miss you let go of last week (or last month, or last year). That's the Spin Cycle.

Mirror connections make it difficult to stay away. Even as the self-correcting nature of the Mirror effect leads you to release a near miss, the same gravity that formed the relationship can continue to exert a force, causing the relationship to re-form. Once re-formed, the relationship might work for a while, but the self-correcting nature will again catch up and the relationship will once again be released. The Spin Cycle is a syndrome that can continue for long periods, especially when you're feeling down. Eventually, though, the Spin Cycle will burn itself out.

Remember, there is a true Magical Match out there for you. Don't waste your time in the spin cycle when you could be finding the relationship of your life!

HOW TO LET GO GRACEFULLY

One of the most important lessons about letting go is that it is *not* about the other individual being a "bad catch"; they're just not *your* Magical Match. For someone else, your Mirror *will be* a Magical Match. There is no reason to assign blame or feel guilty. Letting go means releasing a less than perfect *pairing*. You are both Magical Matchers searching for that magical relationship.

In Mirror dating, letting go means: "This pairing just isn't quite right. You're not getting the best parts of me. You and I both deserve someone who will bring out the best within us. What we have is good, but it will be so much better when you find your Magical Match." If your Mirror is experienced enough in the process, they will likely agree. Knowing that you both deserve better, and that no one was in the wrong, will enable you to recover more quickly.

As Renee explains, the loss of her first Mirror, which initially felt like an insurmountable tragedy, ultimately freed her to find the relationship she'd always wanted:

When I met Jason, I could not believe the strength and intensity of our connection. Coming out of a 28-year marriage, where we were always trying to cram a round peg into a square hole, my relationship with Jason was a shift into a whole different paradigm. Being with him woke up the memory of what I'd always dreamed of and known deep down in my soul to be possible. Our relationship gave me a taste of something so profoundly deep and connected, it was almost out of this world. There was all this connection and all these compatibilities; I had never had anything remotely like that before.

But for various reasons, my love with Jason was not meant to be lived out in a permanent, committed relationship. Within our love, there were things we could control and on the other side of that, there was a vast ocean we could never swim in together. It was a relationship in which we could grow, as well as learn to let go.

When Jason and I decided to terminate our engagement, I wept in his arms for nearly seven hours straight. There had been no fight or harsh words, no battling of the minds. There was however, the strong, silent, mysterious boundary of our love. And like all boundaries that are there for our best, sometimes we cannot see or understand their purpose and value in the moment. Especially when those boundaries fly in the face of our strongest desires. Since I had never known a love of this magnitude, naturally I wanted to cling there.

The closer you get to finding your true mate, the more difficult it gets to let go of a relationship that isn't just right— because the relationship—the one that isn't perfect—is just off-the-charts amazing. My relationship with Jason was so far beyond anything I'd ever experienced that everything else paled in comparison. And after experiencing a love like that, I knew I could never settle for anything less.

It was absolutely excruciating to connect in such a profound way, to be brought to life in a way that I'd never been brought to life before—and then to be told I couldn't have the relationship. It was a pain unlike any other; I was letting go of the most magical, mysterious, profound connection I'd ever had, all the while not knowing if I'd ever have another connection like it.

Thank God, Jason was willing to hold me and let me mourn. And as he held me, he kept saying, "Renee, trust me. There's someone so much better than me coming." He had this uncanny intuition—he knew that there was someone even better out there for both of us. But I couldn't hear it then. I didn't want to hear it. I was in love in a way I'd never been in love before and I couldn't bear to let him go.

But you know what? I'm glad I let go of him—because my relationship with Jason was only a foreshadowing of what I have now. Jason was right. What I have with Erik is even more incredible than what I had with Jason. Erik and I have a more mature, balanced, grounded, complete union. It's more profound and more right for me. The two of us are on a spiritual journey that is more amazing than anything I ever dreamed of, and there's nothing on earth like that.—Renee

A FINAL NOTE ABOUT LETTING GO

With all this connecting and then having to let go, you could easily assume that the experience of losing any number of Mirror connections would erode confidence. Most certainly, this pattern seems endemic to traditional daters. Unlike the traditional dating experience, however, the Mirroring process is filled with connection; these are relationships of deep substance. Although there can be overwhelming sadness and sense of loss, the practice of letting go and finding again actually makes Mirror daters *stronger and more confident in their quest.* When we discover that it is possible to find another, closer match, our fears ease up. Letting go becomes easier. In finding more than one Mirror, we begin to believe that we actually have a *pool* of Mirrors. With increased confidence comes the ability to consciously select a better pairing—there is no need to settle when you *know* that it's possible to have the precise relationship you desire.

Key Concepts

- The near miss and Magical Match have almost equal gravity and connection.
- It is difficult to let go of relationships that are uber-compelling.
- You must quickly let go of the near misses in order to reach your Magical Match.
- Letting Go is about the *pairing* not being as good as it should be.
- As opposed to tearing you down, the Mirroring Process makes you a more a confident dater.

Mirror Effect Laws

- Sometimes love is not enough.
- You only get to discover whether a partner is truly ready to be your Magical Match after you're already deeply involved.
- It's devastating to lose a Mirror relationship. There is no way around it.
- Once you've experienced a Mirror relationship, nothing else will ever do.

Steps Towards Your Magical Match

- Listen to your inner self and Let Go when it is time.
- Pay attention to the Mirror Effect Laws. They are a guide.
- Let Go as gently as possible.
- Allow yourself to grieve the loss before moving on—but not too long.
- Carry on towards your committed goal. Know that another Mirror awaits.

- Update your profile with anything new that you see as a mirror of you. Continue to refine your reflection so that the Mirrors who arrive will be the highest possible matching.
- Seek assistance if you continually fail and don't feel like you're getting better at the process.
- Don't give up on love. Love *will* find a way, just with a different Mirror.
- Don't let a Death Spiral get out of control. Talk with your Mirror about what's up for you.

Letting Go Checklist
- Is there a lack of ease? Does something just feel not quite right, not quite harmonious or easy?
- Has an aspect of the relationship become work?
- Is your Mirror experiencing walls that he/she just can't seem to surmount?
- Are there weaknesses: jealously, insecurity, inability to open or surrender, fear, clinginess?
- Are you waiting for something to improve or be revealed? Chasing potential is a bad idea.
- Have you recently discovered something new about your Mirror that changes the balance within the relationship?
- Are the levels of Mirroring balanced and strong enough?
- Do you feel the need to Let Go?

14

STEP 8 – COMMITMENT
Make it a Mission

Mirroring is a simple and effective process for finding superlative matches–the pinnacle of relationships–but it only works if you commit to the entire process

Marguerite is a good friend. I met her after my divorce. Come to think of it, we met on a date. It wasn't a good relationship pairing, so it was back to the pool.

As I went off on the adventure of discovering Mirroring, Marguerite continued to try and find the love of her life. She had known, and lost, deep love before. And, when I listened carefully, I could see that she didn't believe love would come again. Regardless, she was an online dater seeking someone who matched her well and with whom she could be happy. Nothing grandiose. Happy would do nicely. So Marguerite dated, but there was always something that wasn't just right, and so Marguerite would start again.

Despite—or perhaps because of—her history, Marguerite had an intuitive wisdom about relationships. So I suggested that she try Mirroring. She had watched my near misses, observing my triumph, frustration, and yes, even heartbreak. She also witnessed my ever-building confidence that eventually led me to Judy. Even though Marguerite could see the strength of my Mirrors, she was reluctant to try the process for herself. Eventually, though, she relented.

Our first attempt at Step 1, creating Marguerite's Mirror Profile, was pretty good—and she improved it over time. Her dating experiences, based on her new profile and Mirror-quality dates, provided information that helped her refine her profile and enhance her Mirroring Process. All she needed to do was *commit* to dating only those who matched her profile.

Unfortunately, Marguerite wasn't quite on the same page as me. Even though she had a Mirror Profile, she was not yet a true Magical Matcher. Marguerite continued to date anyone who looked interesting, with little regard for filtering. And the results showed; because her pattern of dating didn't change, neither did the results.

Finally, Marguerite decided to really commit to the Mirror dating process. Almost immediately after making this commitment, Ron appeared. Suddenly, Marguerite was a smiling, happy convert with a loving, harmonious, easy relationship. Within three months, they were living together and have been inseparable ever since. Over the years, Marguerite had given me grief about my theories of Mirrors and now the shoe was on the other foot, and I couldn't be happier for her.

Marguerite's results were quite spectacular, and in a short amount of time. For her to be able to find her Magical Match on the first try was amazing. *But it would never have happened if she hadn't fully committed to the process.*

Committing to the 6 steps sets the stage for the deepest possible connection. Isn't that what you're really looking for?

At 48, I became engaged for the first time. In Troy, I found the man who I had always been looking for. Troy inspires me to greatness. We are so well matched that my only work in the relationship is to open my heart as wide and deep as I can, to become as present as I can, and from there, to focus on all we are and all we create together. Our work is not to make the relationship work or to smooth out mismatched places. Instead, it is to create and bring our gifts to the world.—Judy

WHAT DOES IT TAKE?

Those committed to finding their Magical Match:

- **Know the difference between Mirroring and mass marketing**. A profile should only be changed to increase the quality of matches.
- **Date *only* those who strongly see themselves in the Mirror** created by the words of the profile. Filtering to date only the well-matched makes dating more connected, and with connection comes ease and confidence.
- **Select for relationship only those who are highly matched**—those with whom there is a deep connection, tranquility, and clarity.
- **Release relationships that require work**. When there is a mismatch in Mirror pairing, there is always another, better matched partner.
- **Commit to the process**, and take the time to find your Magical Match by dating, exploring, and learning.

Those who are committed to the 6 Steps will achieve their goal of an amazing, life-altering relationship. Is that not worth the adventure?

Key Concepts
- The only way to find a Magical Match is to commit to the 6-step process. Following the process leads to better dates, more connection, increased confidence, and a clearer understanding of pairing and selection.

Mirror Effect Law
- Effort is required if you want to find your Magical Match.

Steps Towards Your Magical Match
- Make it a mission. Don't settle for any less than a Magical Match.

EPILOGUE

THE FUTURE OF MIRRORING

Infinite Possibilities

Mirroring represents a new frontier. As we step forward with an entirely new way of dating and the different type of relationship it brings, Magical Matchers stand at the forefront of a unique intersection of time, technology, process, and enlightenment—all aligned and working together to help singles find lasting, effortless, deep love. Harnessing the power of the Mirror Effect is the most dramatic, far-reaching change in the way we seek relationships since we started mating for love.

Yet, like a scientist who's made a revolutionary breakthrough, we've just scratched the surface. We have yet to discover all of the intricacies of the Mirror Effect. Certainly we will discover more laws and design new best practices. We will also continue to learn more about the Mirror relationship's vulnerabilities, such as speed and pressure, and catalog mirror pairings as they evolve across time.

And like that scientist, there are new frontiers in which to apply our discovery. Until now, we've worked only with heterosexual pairings, but we expect the Mirroring process to work equally well with gay, lesbian, and other couples. Certainly Mirroring will function well for the baby boomers who have reached an age of wisdom in relationships, but we wonder if young adults will seek something deeper—something beyond the current "hook-up" culture. And how will cultures who tend towards arranged marriage be influenced by Mirroring? Discovering the unique ways the Mirror Effect plays out in all of these situations will continue to shape our understanding of this powerful relationship.

We're also aware that people will adapt this process in the way that best suits *their* needs. Some pairings will contain Mirroring traits mixed with complementary traits. Others will seek traditional pairings with a greater level of mirroring. What unique rewards and challenges will these mixed relationships hold? Together, these are questions we will investigate, follow, and analyze.

Like any new, profound turning point, research and discovery will promote a greater understanding and awareness. As we learn more, our methodology will improve. We will discover new ways to filter and Mirror, new ways to utilize the power of the Internet to help us search for and find our Mirrors. Even more, we will change the meaning of the word "relationship." The very nature of our core beliefs of relationship as the "averaging of misery" will eventually be rewritten with the power of Mirror love. Those who undertake this journey and find success will inevitably change the fabric of our culture.

In reality, it is a change already under way; I have witnessed it with my own eyes. I have personally experienced closed hearts opening. I have seen Mirror love overflow into the broken relationships between parents and children, and seen the contentious relationships of former spouses brought back to understanding and sweet friendship. I have seen the healing power of Mirror love replace profound sorrow with joyous happiness. There is no doubt in my mind: The ability of Mirror love to perform *miracles* is unquestionably real.

And now, it's your turn to begin this remarkable path of discovery. You, too, can experience the deep joy of love and the amazing, profound Mirror relationship that Judy and I share.

AFTERWORD

A THERAPIST'S PERSPECTIVE ON MIRRORING

Stefanie Elkin, MA, LMFT

In my role as a Licensed Marriage and Family Therapist, I've spent the past nearly thirty years working with couples and individuals. Some of my most challenging, yet meaningful work, has been with couples who come in for help as a last-ditch effort to save a long-term, long-faltering relationship. Many of these couples have approached me when their marriages were already in their end stage, barely gasping out their last breaths. Exhausted by empty marriages, the couples came to me, hoping I could miraculously breathe life back into a relationship one or both of them had abandoned long ago.

During initial sessions, it often became apparent that *these relationships suffered from inherent mismatches that were evident right from the early stages of dating.* My inquiries about their initial strengths, attractions, and difficulties prompted them to reflect on problematic issues they had ignored or overlooked when they first met. *No one had ever taught them how to successfully choose a partner.* And so they married.

Other clients, already dating or in established relationships, were desperately trying to mold their partners into "the One." From my perspective, I could see that, in all likelihood, it would never work; the couple was too mismatched. But their desire to be together overrode the wisdom of being discerning.

And so they kept reading self-help books, attending seminars, and coming to therapy. They insisted they wanted to work it out, because the good parts felt good and the painful or missing parts "just needed more work." In my extensive years of clinical experience, "more work" is rarely enough to overcome deep mismatches at the core.

Rather than pay attention to the inherent flaws in the relationship, these couples worked tirelessly to force their partners to embody the characteristics they'd always wanted in a spouse. To my clinical eye, the differences between the fantasy and the reality posed too wide a chasm. "To make this work," I wanted to tell them, "You need to be somebody else." But these are not words a therapist can say.

My agenda for married couples, especially those with children, is to help bridge the mismatches, improving the relationship enough to keep it intact and make it a decent environment in which to raise the children. I advise each member of the couple to give it their absolute best, and if that does not turn out to be workable or satisfying enough, based on their own measures, to end it.

Naturally, I advise singles quite differently. Daters—or people exploring new relationships—needn't work that hard. Trying to squeeze your date into the preconceived mold you carry in your mind's eye means they have to be liquefied first. This always turns out poorly.

One day last year, I got a call from my good friend Judy Day. At 48, Judy had never married. Over the years, I watched her date a number of men who seemed great on paper, at least at first. But as the relationships unfolded and matured, there were always aspects that were unsuitable for long-term partnerships—too much of this or too little of that. Since Judy had no agenda to get married, she often stayed in these relationships too long, hoping that things might improve with time. "It's not great," she'd say to me, "but I'm learning a lot, so there's value in that, right?" Well, sure....

Now, Judy was calling to tell me about another new man. This time, though, I heard something different in her voice—and in her whole being. It instantly caught my attention, so much so that at the end of our conversation, I challenged her, "You're going to marry this guy, aren't you?"

It was a crazy thing for me to ask; I believe love needs to be time-tested. But I was testing *her*. Judy was grounded and stable in her enthusiasm and excitement in a way I had never known her to be in the past. There was a security and clarity in her description of Troy that was both noteworthy and astonishing. So I wasn't fully surprised when she answered my question with a slow certainty that surprised even her: "You know what, I think I will."

A month later, Judy hosted a small dinner party to let her close friends meet Troy. I was intrigued and eager to meet this new man of hers, to see for myself what she might be deluding herself into. My bullshit meter was on full throttle.

The moment I walked in the door and saw him, I *knew* immediately. Troy was tall, statuesque, and striking—just like Judy. He introduced himself and I shook hands with him. His energy was dynamic, potent, and vibrant—just like Judy. *He felt like a male version of her.* We hadn't even had a conversation, yet it was already clear to me that he and Judy were exceptionally well matched.

And matching my friend Judy was no easy task. A successful businesswoman, Judy has a very bold personality and is highly independent. Troy was the first man Judy had ever been with who could fully meet her, love her in her boldness, and support her in becoming *even more of whom she was meant to be.*

Judy and Troy became engaged in a short period of time. Being in their presence was fascinating. Together, they behaved as though they were well-rehearsed musicians. Fluid, at ease, gracefully integrated—like a couple that had been together for decades. Being in their presence was inspiring.

When we met, Troy was already writing this book—a book about the process he had used to find Judy. This was highly intriguing to me, since the obvious results were impressive. I had deemed the quality of their pairing extremely rare—or just plainly lucky.

Over the course of a few dinners, we discussed his new methodology, which he claimed could reproduce the same quality of matching that he shared with Judy.

As I began to think of about the ramifications of a streamlined approach to dating that produced incredibly well matched partnerships, I got excited. What intrigued me most was that Troy's theories and methodologies readily fit into the clinical models I'd been teaching throughout my career.

I have consistently worked with clients developing their consciousness and skill levels for relational discernment. I've encouraged them to pay attention, not only to the strengths of a new relationship, but to its weaknesses as well. This has never been popular with clients; no one ever wants me to rain on their parade. Few clients heeded my warnings—especially when they were newly into relationships where a poor fit was already apparent. Or when finding someone good-looking was reason enough to start dating. But my message has always remained the same: "Focus on finding relationships that are highly compatible. Get out of those that are not."

When I talked to Troy and Judy about my work, they were excited by the commonalities in our thinking. When they asked me to join the project, I was honored to participate. I had worked with these concepts for decades. Now, finally, here was a way they could be taught: *a system for creating great pairings.*

It has become clear to me that the implications of The Mirror Effect are far greater than I first imagined. What would happen if millions of couples moved forward lovingly through life together without inherent drama, conflict, or separation? What would it mean for children to be raised in intact families by couples that have the emotional wherewithal to nurture and support, rather than cope and survive?

I am excited to be at the forefront of this new movement. I look forward to the research that will be done on the specific and overarching results of this new methodology. We will all be pioneers together, learning, modifying, and refining where needed. I hope your enthusiasm comes to match mine, and that you join us in exploring the full potential of The Mirror Effect.

Stefanie Elkin, LMFT

ABOUT MAGICALMATCHES.COM

Now that you've learned about the power, possibilities and potential of The Mirror Effect, it's your turn. Use the promotional code on page 148 to find your Magical Match at MagicalMatches.com

Online dating has opened new doors in the way we search for love, but it needs to do more than just match subscribers to the expiration dates on their credit cards. Online dating must evolve. It must grow beyond the need for people to market themselves or answer a zillion questions to satisfy "the machine." It must evolve to actually produce results for the vast majority of its subscribers, and most importantly, it must deliver pairings that are more than the same old, traditional relationship.

When we discovered the Mirror Effect and Mirroring, it became immediately apparent that implementing these concepts would intrinsically produce a dating site that was vastly different to the status quo—one that could actually accomplish the task of bringing the deepest love to those serious about finding long-term relationships.

Here's why MagicalMatches.com is the new standard in Online Dating:

It's super easy to get started

On MagicalMatches.com there are no personal profiles, so you don't have to write one! There's no long, tedious list of questions you have to answer. Instead, with our patent-pending process, you read a set of Mirror profiles written about the heart, soul, and mind. Selecting the one that most clearly Mirrors you places you in a pool alongside others who share your Mirror elements, your deepest characteristics. Without having to write a single word, you've already completed Step 1 and performed the first stage filter! All that's left is for you to upload a few pictures and enter your logistics into your Mirror Page.

It's simple to filter down to your Magical Match

We calculate a Mirror Index for each person in your Mirror Pool, automatically providing a second level of filtering. Now that the best Mirrors for you are filtered and sorted, searching through your Mirror Pool is quick and easy. Instead of reading hundreds of individual profiles to find someone you want to meet, you can see a picture of each person in your pool and quickly review their Keys to the Heart, Deal Makers and Breakers, Feedback, etc. Within 60 seconds you'll know everything you need to decide whether this person has Mirror potential for you. One step closer to your goal....

You're in control of the machine

People are more than just machines matched by mathematics. Even as we know that an exact Mirror represents the greatest chance for long-term success, it does no good to have a 100% Mirror match to someone who is outside your personal likes—the human factor must not be ignored. So, we've built a method for you to personalize your Mirror Index by simply liking or disliking something you see on a Mirror page. Think what Pandora does for music. If you are viewing someone else's mirror page, you can like their age, or where he lives, her religion, or anything else on the page. Each time you like or dislike something, that selection is added to your personal dating genome. This dating genome, unique to MagicalMatches.com, enables you to hone in on the Mirrors who best fit your likes and dislikes.

We provide tools for the Mirroring Process

Our job doesn't end when you send the first email. No way! We provide you the tools to help you recognize the emphatic email response from the drivel so you know when to date. Our questionnaires and checklists will help you understand whether your date was a Mirror. Right on the website, you'll be able to graph each of the Mirror Elements so you can *quantitatively measure* that amazing Mirror connection and relationship.

We've built Magical Matches so that you'll be able to easily focus on the levels of mirroring to ensure that you efficiently Filter, Connect, and Select your way to your Magical Match.

The Magical Matcher's User Community

It's the era of social networking, so we've built it in. But it's not social for social's sake. We've brought only the pieces of social that make sense for your dating experience.

- **Feedback**

  Let's be honest. We've all been on that date where someone isn't quite what they claimed in their profile. I'm not talking about his hair being different than his online pictures, or that she wore something different to the date. Rather it's more like he doesn't have hair anymore and her pictures were from her college years.

  Most people are fantastic and honest, and those are the people we want as Magical Matchers. When you've experienced a wonderful person for a date, you'll be able to post that feedback for others to see. If the pictures were 20 years old, you'll be able to post that feedback too.

  We believe that a few bad apples spoil the fun for everyone. With community feedback, the bad apples will find a different online dating site, leaving a better dating pool from which to Filter and Select on the journey to finding the love of your life.

- **Get help from your friends**

  Who knows you better than your friends? Why not bring your friends to your online dating experience. Most of us do anyway, right? Who hasn't shown the profile of tonight's date to a friend to see what they think?

  So, we decided that it would be fun to be able to let your friends in on the experience. With our social network feature, you can decide to invite your friends to look at your Mirror Pool and vote on those they think would be good (or bad) matches. And just like in real life, you can ask friends in your social network to introduce you to someone you're interested in. Additionally, your friends can vouch for your excellent character and sharp wit by leaving a recommendation for you—just another part of the community feedback.

We will continue to support you every step of the way!

Any online dating site can write articles about dating or blog the latest research in relationships. But does that *really* help you in finding your match?

At MagicalMatches.com we talk to our subscribers every day—*live*. Through conference calls and webinars, our goal is to help 10,000 Magical Matchers a day to understand the Mirror Effect, Mirror dating and relationships, website usage and features—anything and everything. Whether you're wondering, "Is it normal that she feels like a female version of me" or "Is it supposed to go this fast?" or "How do I adjust my dating genome?"—no matter the question, there's an online *meeting* to answer it! We're here to guide you through each of the 6 steps on your way to finding your effort-less, harmonious, magical love story.

It's about you, not us. We promise.

On Magical Matches there is no advertising. We don't auto-renew credit card charges (unless that's what you want). We won't leave you to figure out how things work on your own. Actually, it's quite the opposite. We promise to do whatever we can to ensure that you find your Magical Match. Period.

We put our money where our mouth is.

To help you get started on your way to the relationship for a life-time, your first month is on us. Just enter the promotional code *TheDeepEnd* on the sign up page to become a member of our excit-ing community.

Come find your Magical Match at www.magicalmatches.com.

Welcome To Deep End Of The Dating Pool

ABOUT THE AUTHORS

TROY PUMMILL Troy's background as an innovator, inventor, consultant, and entrepreneur brings forth a level of undeniable expertise in his industry. Troy has spent his entire 25-year career in Silicon Valley working for and consulting to start-up network equipment manufacturers with a specialty in network protocols. A non-conformist, his knack for recognizing patterns and creating unconventional solutions has led to numerous innovative applications, features and several patents, including a patent for breaking into encrypted computer communications—a mathematically impossible task. Troy is also an experienced trainer and staunch customer service advocate.

A veteran of 20 years of marriage that resulted in a divorce, Troy was led to an experience that profoundly opened his eyes to seeing *relationships* in a radically different way. He spent three years researching and experiencing what became The Mirror Effect. Troy combined his epic journey of marriage and three years of Mirror Effect online dating with his expertise in patterns and protocols to define the Mirror relationship paradigm, The Magical Matches online dating website, and ultimately, the 6 Steps to Finding your Magical Match.

JUDY DAY Judy is a CEO, innovator of her market segment, patent holder, and entrepreneur. Judy started her manufacturing company with $500 and a desire to ease people's pain. Twenty years later she deftly handles one of the most complex business operations, which includes offshore manufacturing and direct sales to retail chains including Bed, Bath, and Beyond; TJ Max; Kmart; Safeway; as well as more than 3,000 individual retailers worldwide.

As a former ICU Nurse, Judy ran a high altitude hospital at the base of Mount Everest and now because of the Mirror Effect, she has the Everest of relationships. Judy brings her two decades of business experience and analytical strength to Magical Matches and The Mirror Effect. Judy is not only responsible for writing portions of the book, but also was agent provocateur behind codifying the 6 step process. She is also the lead researcher on creating the profiles for the MagicalMatches.com, a daunting, but crucial, sojourn into questions of the heart, soul, and mind that philosophers and scientists have been trying to define for thousands of years.